Editor-in-Chief and Founder:
Lyndon H. LaRouche, Jr.
Editorial Board: *Lyndon H. LaRouche, Jr. , Helga Zepp-LaRouche, Robert Ingraham, Tony Papert, Gerald Rose, Dennis Small, Jeffrey Steinberg, William Wertz*
Co-Editors: *Robert Ingraham, Tony Papert*
Technology: *Marsha Freeman*
Books: *Katherine Notley*
Ebooks: *Richard Burden*
Graphics: *Alan Yue*
Photos: *Stuart Lewis*
Circulation Manager: *Stanley Ezrol*

INTELLIGENCE DIRECTORS
Counterintelligence: *Jeffrey Steinberg, Michele Steinberg*
Economics: *John Hoefle, Marcia Merry Baker, Paul Gallagher*
History: *Anton Chaitkin*
Ibero-America: *Dennis Small*
Russia and Eastern Europe: *Rachel Douglas*
United States: *Debra Freeman*

INTERNATIONAL BUREAUS
Bogotá: *Miriam Redondo*
Berlin: *Rainer Apel*
Copenhagen: *Tom Gillesberg*
Houston: *Harley Schlanger*
Lima: *Sara Madueño*
Melbourne: *Robert Barwick*
Mexico City: *Gerardo Castilleja Chávez*
New Delhi: *Ramtanu Maitra*
Paris: *Christine Bierre*
Stockholm: *Ulf Sandmark*
United Nations, N.Y.C.: *Leni Rubinstein*
Washington, D.C.: *William Jones*
Wiesbaden: *Göran Haglund*

ON THE WEB
e-mail: eirns@larouchepub.com
www.larouchepub.com
www.executiveintelligencereview.com
www.larouchepub.com/eiw
Webmaster: *John Sigerson*
Assistant Webmaster: *George Hollis*
Editor, Arabic-language edition: *Hussein Askary*

EIR (ISSN 0273-6314) *is published weekly (50 issues), by EIR News Service, Inc., P.O. Box 17390, Washington, D.C. 20041-0390. (703) 297-8434*

European Headquarters: E.I.R. GmbH, Postfach Bahnstrasse 9a, D-65205, Wiesbaden, Germany
Tel: 49-611-73650
Homepage: http://www.eir.de
e-mail: info@eir.de
Director: Georg Neudecker

Montreal, Canada: 514-461-1557
eir@eircanada.ca

Denmark: EIR - Denmark, Sankt Knuds Vej 11, basement left, DK-1903 Frederiksberg, Denmark.
Tel.: +45 35 43 60 40, Fax: +45 35 43 87 57. e-mail: eirdk@hotmail.com.

Mexico City: EIR, Sor Juana Inés de la Cruz 242-2 Col. Agricultura C.P. 11360 Delegación M. Hidalgo, México D.F.
Tel. (5525) 5318-2301
eirmexico@gmail.com

Copyright: ©2017 EIR News Service. All rights reserved. Reproduction in whole or in part without permission strictly prohibited.

Canada Post Publication Sales Agreement #40683579

Postmaster: Send all address changes to *EIR*, P.O. Box 17390, Washington, D.C. 20041-0390.

Signed articles in *EIR* represent the views of the authors, and not necessarily those of the Editorial Board.

The New Way to Infrastructure and Jobs

EIR Contents

www.larouchepub.com Volume 45, Number 7, February 16, 2018

Cover This Week

Workers at the construction site of a tram system in Yunnan Province, China, May 27, 2016.

THE NEW WAY TO INFRASTRUCTURE AND JOBS

I. The World Has Changed Dramatically

II. The Unity of Science and Art

III. LaRouche on Scientific-Moral Principle

ZEPP-LAROUCHE FEB. 8 WEBCAST

Consolidate the New Paradigm, Now That the British Coup Against Trump Is Exposed

Helga Zepp-LaRouche's weekly webcast of Feb. 8 can be seen at newparadigm.schillerinstitute.com. *The transcript has been edited.*

Harley Schlanger: Hello! I'm Harley Schlanger for the Schiller Institute, Welcome to this week's strategic webcast by Helga Zepp-LaRouche, founder of the Schiller Institutes.

There's a breaking situation in the United States, Helga, which is really quite astonishing. I think it's worth noting that since the role of the British is now finally coming into focus—the role the British played in setting up the whole operation against the Trump Presidency. Back in November and December 2016, when the operation against Trump was just beginning, you and your husband emphasized that if the operation was going to be stopped, it had to be done by going after the British role, not just in running the operation, but by exposing what was being protected by trying to knock out Trump. I think you have the latest developments on this: Why don't you give us the picture?

Helga Zepp-LaRouche: The plot is thickening, as they say. Actually the story is really unbelievable, and I'm quite proud that I wrote an article at the very beginning of this affair, where I said there is collusion with the British and not with Russia—and that is exactly what is now coming out, and it's becoming a subject in the public domain. So, I'll start with the multimillin dollar libel case against Christopher Steele, the allegedly "former" MI6 agent. The case was

supposed to be tried in the High Court in London. Steele was supposed to appear for a deposition, but then at the last minute was represented instead by his lawyer, the argument being that this could touch on British national security interests. And, lo and behold, a representative of the Foreign Office was also there, with Foreign Office lawyers, stating the same thing.

So the role of the British government, British intelligence, is now a subject in the get-Trump operation. It is quite clear that Christopher Steele is not some random former MI6 agent, but that he is, indeed, an asset not only of the British, but also of the FBI. This point has come out in a very interesting article on Pat Lang's blog, "Sic Semper Tyrannis."

Sic Semper Tyrannis

Colonel Pat Lang's Outpost - "A Committee of Correspondence"

07 FEBRUARY 2018

Did British Intelligence Try to Destroy the Trump Presidency? by Publius Tacitus

Last night's release of the memo by Senator's Grassley and Graham asking the Department of Justice to open a criminal investigation of Christopher Steele for possible violations of 18 U.S.C. § 1001 provides critical confirmation of charges presented in the HPSCI memo prepared under the leadership of Devin Nunes, but it also confirms that Christopher Steele was not just some random guy offering good gossip to the FBI. He was an official intelligence asset. He was, in John LeCarre's parlance, our ".Joe." At least we

A regular, respected contributor to that blog, who posts there under the pseudonym "Publius Tacitus," asks in his headline, "Did British Intelligence Try To Destroy the Trump Presidency?" which is exactly what we are looking at. The host of this blog, Col. Patrick Lang—for most people who don't know him—is a senior retired officer of U.S. Military Intelligence and U.S. Army Special Forces (the Green Berets), not at all some Russian or some other source which might be questioned in this context, but he worked for the Defense Intelligence Agency for a long time, and he's very respected.

"Publius Tacitus" points to the fact that the new memos which have come out from Senator Grassley and Senator Graham, and the Senate Homeland Security and Government Affairs Committee all corroborate what is in the Nunes House Intelligence memorandum. And indeed, there are a lot of new aspects. They imply that maybe former FBI Director James Comey lied under oath, because when he gave the famous press conference exonerating Hillary Clinton, he claimed that he had not coordinated that with anybody else. That is in stark contradiction to some other texts that were exchanged between Peter Strzok and Lisa Page, two FBI officials, who were involved in both the email affair of Hillary Clinton and also in Russiagate which indicate that Hillary knew that there would be no charges against her. So, that needs further investigation.

Then, another very ominous sign has appeared, and that is another text exchange between these two: They say on Sept. 2, 2016, that "POTUS" that is, the "President of the United States," namely Obama, wanted to know everything they are doing. Now, what does this "everything" refer to? Either it refers to the Hillary Clinton investigation, or else to Russiagate, and the latter would mean that Obama is now directly tied to Russiagate—not only indirectly through the payment of Fusion GPS and Steele, where the Obama Administration also paid, along with the DNC and the Hillary Clinton campaign.

This is all extremely, extremely hot, and there are now all these Senate and Congressional hearings and committees investigating this. Congressman Nunes,

Former FBI Director James Comey testifying and Victoria Nuland, both under fire.

who had published this memo—or President Trump had agreed to having it declassified and published last Friday—said this is only "Phase 1." There are more phases to come, and they will involve, among other things, the State Department—and that of course also involves Victoria Nuland, whose name has now come up. And there was also, on another matter, many exchanges between Christopher Steele and Victoria Nuland in respect to the coup in Ukraine, the infamous February 2014 Maidan coup.

This is all very interesting, very hot. Russiagate is practically a dead letter, but what is now on the table instead, is the meddling of the British government, British intelligence, in the election in the United States, trying to sabotage the Trump victory, first, and when he won anyway, to destroy the Trump Presidency with a completely fabricated accusation. This is now out in the open, and this is big! And I am still absolutely shocked and surprised—even though this has been going on for some time—at the way the mainstream Western media has managed not to cover this, when it is clearly reaching dimensions which go far, far beyond Watergate.

Schlanger: What we are getting from the media and from the anti-Trump forces, are screams of protest. And in fact, it's interesting: They took the word that was used originally to describe Russiagate, that is, "a nothingburger," to try to attribute that to Nunes's report, saying it's a "nothingburger." But the fact that you heard nothing but "nothingburger, nothingburger, nothingburger," shows you that they're coordinating a response where they have nothing else to say! So it's a nothingburger about a nothingburger.

I think the other thing that's important, Helga, is that the *Washington Post* came out Feb. 6, and identified the key role of Sir Richard Dearlove, the former head of MI6, and a great supporter of Steele; this, combined with the Foreign Office showing up yesterday in court to protect him, makes it unmistakably clear that this is a high-level British intelligence operation.

Zepp-LaRouche: Yes. As a matter of fact, the article on Pat Lang's blog, which I just mentioned, pointed to redacted places in the memo, and some which were not redacted, and the author, being knowledgeable in intelligence, points to a reference made to a form called "FD-1023," which is an FBI form to document debriefings of FBI sources; and he concludes that this meant that Steele was in some kind of a source relation to the FBI, and that raises questions—did his superiors know? If not, this may cause big legal problems for Christopher Steele in working for a foreign intelligence agency, being a so-called "former" MI6 agent himself, but more likely with approval or actually under the direction of MI6.

And the fact that Richard Dearlove, the former head of MI6, completely defended the reputation of Steele, is very interesting in this respect, because who is this Dearlove? He is the author of the famous dossier which led to the attack on Iraq in the Second Gulf War, supposedly because Saddam Hussein was in the possession of weapons of mass destruction—which we know was a blatant lie. It was that which led Colin Powell to make his infamous speech at the United Nations in February

Sir Richard Dearlove, head of the British Secret Intelligence Service, MI6, from 1999 to May 6, 2004.

2003, which he later characterized as the biggest mistake of his life, because it led to the war against Saddam Hussein. And there are recent studies, which I think need to be mentioned, which show that in the last 27 years, since the Second Iraq War, 329 people have died in that region every day, either in Afghanistan, Pakistan, Iraq, Syria, Yemen, Libya or elsewhere, because of these wars. That policy must eventually also be brought to trial. And I know that Attorney General Ramsey Clark tried, at the time, to make that an issue before international legal authorities.

So this is not just a coup attempt against the United States, but it is a paradigm of the policies which have led to the present condition of the world, including the destruction of much of Southwest Asia, including the refugee crisis. So these are not small things, and I think it is high time that this whole paradigm should come out in the open and be replaced by a completely different policy.

Peace Platform for the 21st Century

Schlanger: The other thing that's important now, is we're beginning to see the role that the media are playing come out in a totally blatant way. There's an op-ed column in the *Washington Post* saying that Trump will learn to fear the FBI the way other Presidents have, referencing what J. Edgar Hoover did to blackmail Presidents, and why does Trump think he can take on the secret services?

The other irony here was pointed out by famous author David Garrow, asking why is it that liberals are cheering the "Deep State"? I think you had a chance to the see the Garrow report. What's the importance of this, in terms of holding a mirror up in front of the so-called "progressive movement" in the United States?

Zepp-LaRouche: And the left and liberals in Europe as well. What Garrow, the author of a biography of Martin Luther King, points out, is that the predecessors of these same Democrats in the Congress sided with the civil rights movement, and not with the FBI at that time, and in the '70s, the Church Committee exposed all of these FBI activities; yet the Democrats today are covering up for it. Garrow says that the reason is that there is such a degree of partisan hatred against Trump, that it makes these people blind to what is going on.

Now, I think this will lead to a big crisis of identity, because I don't think that everyone will fall for this. More voices will come out and point to the fact, as Paul Craig Roberts did, that if these people were to win, the United States would become a complete police dictatorship under the control of the secret services—and who would want that?

So, I think the stakes here are extremely high, and people should look at the material which is coming out, and really rethink everything, because it is an unbelievable scandal.

Schlanger: One other footnote on the media: You now have John Brennan, the murderous former CIA director, who has just been hired as a commentator for NBC, and then a top aide to former FBI Director James Comey, former countertorrorism expert Phil Mudd, was hired by CNN. This is somewhat unprecedented, wouldn't you say?

Zepp-LaRouche: Well—we knew that from the former G.D.R. (East Germany), there was something called the "black channel"— weekly political propaganda programs— so people knew what a state-controlled media was. But that it's happening in the United States now, in this open fashion, should give people more food for thought.

Schlanger: The other thing people have to look at is the escalation of the attacks on China, which we started talking about two weeks ago. This is reaching a kind of fever-pitch, with participation of Senator Marco Rubio, and the German think-tank MERICS; this is pretty extensive, and I think you should give people a sense of how wild this is.

Zepp-LaRouche: It seems to be an internationally coordinated attack on China and the New Silk Road. For example, the Australian Secret Intelligence Organization (ASIO) put out a report saying that China is an "extreme threat" to the national security of Australia; then you had the commander of the U.S. Pacific Command, Admiral Harry Harris, who said that China was a disturbing factor in the Indo-Pacific region, a "disruptor;" then the European Council on Foreign Relations issued a report Dec. 1, 2017—"China at the Gates: A New Power Audit of EU-China Relations"— attacking Chinese policy. And you have by MERICS, this German think-tank, together with the Global Public Policy Institute (GPPi) which is based in Berlin. When you read their report, which I did, it is very clear that they are really completely freaked out about the fact that China is winning and the West is losing.

If it didn't have such severe strategic consequences, it would almost be amusing, because they find noteworthy, or questionable, or they criticize the fact that for example Greek Prime Minister Alexis Tsipras attended the Belt and Road Forum in Beijing in May 2017 where he praised China and the New Silk Road! What a crime! Or, that President Milos Zeman of the Czech Republic invited Xi Jinping for a state visit—what a crime! Or that the 16+1 Central and Eastern European Countries are very happy to cooperate with the New Silk Road, because it provides them with the kind of infrastructure investment which the EU did not provide. And then, they say that the Chinese policy of the New Silk Road

Admiral Harry Harris (left), commander of the U.S. Pacific Command, speaking with U.S. Secretary of Defense James Mattis, at Hickam Airfield, Pearl Harbor.

places in question the fundamental assumptions about the role of Europe on the world stage—well, [laughs]

I mean, I really couldn't help smiling because it is true! China *is* offering a different system! And there was just a response to all these attacks in the Chinese newspaper *Global Times*, where the article says that what is behind the "China threat" story is the fact that China is, indeed, proposing a different path for the development of human society, and they're proud to say it—and it's true that they have a very different conception.

I find it also quite remarkable that a high-ranking bishop in Rome, at the Vatican, Chancellor of the Pontifical Academy of Sciences, Marcelo Sánchez Sorondo, praised China. He just visited China, to negotiate Church matters between the Catholic Church in China and the Vatican. When he came back this is what he had to say: "Right now, those who are best implementing the social doctrine of the Catholic Church are the Chinese. You don't have shantytowns, you do not have drugs, young people don't take drugs." Instead, there is a "positive national conscience."

The Feb. 6, 2018 *Catholic Herald,* reports Chancellor Sorondo stated: "What I found was an extraordinary China. What people don't realize is that the central value in China is work, work, work. There's no other way; fundamentally it is like St. Paul said: He who doesn't work, doesn't eat."

He went out of his way to praise what he saw in China.

I find that quite amusing, because it's true! China is offering a different model of development. They have the idea of overcoming poverty, and of offering the Chinese model of success to every other country, without imposing their values. They're perfectly happy to accept different social systems. Having studied Chinese history off and on for more than 40 years, I have come to the conclusion that the idea of accusing China of imperialism, is just completely outside of reality, because China is an example of accepting the sovereignty of every other country, and they have made that the absolute basis of the policy of the Belt and Road Initiative—and that is why it is so successful.

In the article in the *Global Times*, they say that all of

Xinhua/Wang Ye

Greek Prime Minister Alexis Tsipras at a plenary session of the the Belt and Road Forum for International Cooperation, in Beijing, China, May 14, 2017.

this China-bashing will not prevent the West from failing, and that some Westerners would rather see the West fail, than agree to accept the fact that the East is rising.

Schlanger: There's a profound irony here, which is that the people who are accusing China of imperial policies are the same ones who are pushing a containment policy against Russia and China, encirclement of Russia and China, and military buildup—this policy is the old geopolitics. The irony here is that while they're doing this and risking war, China is making great progress, with South Europe, Eastern Europe, and also Latin America.

I think there was a very significant development out of Latin America just in the last couple of days.

Zepp-LaRouche: Yes. In a Feb. 1 speech at the University of Texas at Austin, U.S. Secretary of State Rex Tillerson accused China of imperial policies in Latin America. Following the very successful meeting between China and the CELAC countries, (the Latin American and Caribbean countries) he accused China of imperial motives.

Now, it's quite good and interesting that the times in which such frivolous statements would go uncommented upon, obviously are over, because a whole series of ambassadors from various Latin American countries to China, all came out individually absolutely refuting this—saying, no, their countries are cooperating economically with China completely of their own

University of Texas, Austin

U.S. Secretary of State Rex Tillerson (left) at the University of Texas in Austin, Feb. 1, 2018.

free will, that it's very advantageous for both sides, refuting what Tillerson said.

This policy of China is very good. It is a strategic initiative with which, if it were accepted by the United States and by European nations, we would have a platform for peace! If we have win-win cooperation on a global scale, I think that is the way that we can create a platform for a peace and security doctrine for the 21st Century. I think that needs more debate, and I would hope there are more people speaking out, like these Latin American ambassadors, because that's exactly what we need. We need a real, international discourse about the different models of policy, and it should be conducted in a democratic, free spirit, where people can say what they think according to the First Amendment of the American Constitution. We should have a free dialogue about the merits of each system. I think that that would be very healthy for the whole world.

To Solve the Financial Crisis

Schlanger: Helga, in the interest of starting that dialogue, I would like you to comment on the relationship between the financial crisis and the war danger, because we've seen a series of shocks this week, from the stock markets. Whether this is the big crash or not is still to be determined—but all the bubbles are set to crash, although Mario Draghi, the President of the European Central Bank, says he "sees no bubbles!" But the war danger and the financial crisis seem to always march in common, and I think it would be very helpful for people if you discuss why that's the case.

Zepp-LaRouche: Well, first of all, I think we are sitting on the edge of a new financial crash, which could become much, much worse than 2008. Therefore, what Draghi said is just completely absurd. The only explanation for why he would say something like that, is that he must himself be in a bubble which prevents him from seeing the world as it is.

A recent report by the German Banking Association, warns of many dangers, of the overall international debt. There was a relatively big shakeup on Friday, where the markets lost 666 points; on Monday it was 1,203 points, and in only a few days, a nominal value of $4 trillion was just wiped out from the electronic accounting. So, it's not yet the big crash, but it's a precursor of what could happen at any moment.

And I think that the relation to the dangers of war is that the powers that be—Wall Street, the City of London, the military-industrial complex—are people whose privileges are entirely based on the system of maximum profit-seeking, of becoming richer with each wave of quantitative easing, and with pure manipulation of book-values—which is what it is, when a firm takes a loan at zero interest and then buys their own stock, and they are all richer. In reality, this only helps and serves a very small fraction of the population, which becomes richer and richer.

These people are the same ones who are behind Russiagate, the same ones who are behind the idea that Trump must be prevented by all means from cooperating with Russia and China; the same people who insist on beefing up the NATO troops at the Russian border, and who are risking geopolitical confrontations all the time. That their policies are not working, and that all these sanctions and NATO expansion and so forth, have not led to the demise of Putin, nor the demise of Xi Jinping, apparently does not deter them.

The only solution to this financial crisis is the implementation of Glass-Steagall banking separation, with the Four Laws developed by my husband Lyndon LaRouche. Populations of all countries must *demand* that their governments respond to Xi Jinping's offer of cooperating with the New Silk Road. Both Europe and the United States, are in urgent need of infrastructure improvement and modernization. There is plenty of work to do, including in joint ventures in reconstructing Southwest Asia after the wars of destruction. There is an urgent need for everyone to cooperate in the industrialization of Africa, if the refugee crisis is to be solved in a human way. We really need a public discussion and

Xinhua/Yao Dawei

Kim Yong-nam (left), president of the Supreme People's Assembly of the Democratic People's Republic of Korea, welcomed by South Korean President Moon Jae-in and his wife, at the PyeongChang Winter Olympics in South Korea, Feb. 9, 2018.

a public mobilization to avoid these dangers. I think we're very close to a solution; I think the New Paradigm already exists, and it would be very easy for the Western countries to give up their idea of geopolitical manipulation, and instead cooperate on an equal footing with Russia and China. And for anybody who is interested in world peace, that is the only way out of this crisis.

Schlanger: On this question of war and peace, we have the beginning of the Winter Olympics in South Korea Feb. 9-25, which may be the scene of some interesting developments.

Zepp-LaRouche: Well, it is not yet quite clear: I think between the two Koreas, it is going very well, because Kim Yo-jong, the sister of Kim Jong-un is participating, and so is the head of state of North Korea Kim Yong-nam, so there is a very high level delegation from North Korea participating, and one can be pretty sure that between them and the South Korean leader-

ship, there will be good discussions. Unfortunately, U.S. Vice President Mike Pence couldn't find a worse moment than this to demand a hardening of the sanctions against North Korea, rather than using this moment of relative thaw, to try to move things forward. And of course, North Korea immediately answered with a military parade and said they're not going to talk to the Americans. So this is very unfortunate, but let's see how this process between the two Koreas develops. It's a hopeful moment from that standpoint.

Schlanger: I expect to hear from the neocons any time now, that they're considering the North Korean participation in the women's hockey team has to do with hockey sticks as a dual use weapon, or something.

Helga, just to conclude the discussion, I want to come back to the importance of the breakthrough from the Congressional memos focusing on the British. What should people around the world be doing, to make sure that this not just continues, but succeeds in breaking the power of this group of coup-plotters?

Zepp-LaRouche: Circulate the Mueller dossier written by Barbara Boyd and published by LaRouche PAC. This was written half a year ago, but if you read this dossier now, you will found out how absolutely on the mark it is concerning the role of British intelligence. The circulation of this dossier is something everybody can do very easily. Get it into the social media, get it into the alternative blogs, get it into any newspaper which has the honesty to follow events in a truthful way. Right now, things are coming out in the open. There have been articles by Ray McGovern, William Binney, Pat Lang, RT, all of which pick up on the fact that Russiagate is completely falling apart now. So I think the more people can do to get public attention focussed on this absolutely gigantic fight going on in the United States, the better. Because some of these spooks shy away from daylight, and the more the Sun shines on them, the better.

Schlanger: And this is the opportunity to put an end to the dangerous doctrine of geopolitics, which of course was invented by the British.

So, Helga, thank you again for joining us, and we'll see you next week.

Zepp-LaRouche: Yes. Good-bye.

British Controlling Hand In Russiagate Exposed

by Harley Schlanger

Feb. 9—Recent events in the ongoing "Russia-gate" saga in the United States fully confirm what Lyndon and Helga Zepp LaRouche said when the anti-Trumpers first began peddling the "Russia meddled/Trump colluded" fairy tale about the 2016 presidential election: It is not Russia, they charged, but the British who attempted to rig the election, colluding with Obama intelligence agency leaders and the Hillary Clinton campaign to defeat Donald Trump and sabotage his presidency.

To end the coup danger, they added, the British must be exposed, and their operations in the United States must be permanently shut down. With the release of two memos in the last week, by Representative Devin Nunes and Senators Chuck Grassley and Lindsey Graham, focused on the pivotal role of "former" MI6 operative Christopher Steele in the attempted coup against President Donald Trump, there is no longer any doubt that the LaRouches were right.

Christopher Steele is the author of a very dirty dossier on Trump which claims that the President is a pawn of Putin and is subject to Russian blackmail. The dossier, it turns out, was paid for by Hillary Clinton and the Democratic National Committee as part of the work of Fusion GPS, Steele's U.S. partner, in the 2016 election. It was shopped simultaneously through the FBI and other Obama intelligence agencies, and the Clinton Campaign, to the national news media. It was the backbone of the FBI counterintelligence investigation of the Trump campaign which began in July of 2016, and continues to this day under Special Counsel Robert Mueller. According to the Nunes House Intelligence Committee Memo, fired Deputy FBI Director Andrew McCabe told the House Intelligence Committee that there would have been no FISA applications for surveillance concerning the Trump campaign, were it not for this British handiwork.

On Feb. 2, Congressman Nunes, the Chair of the House Permanent Subcommittee on Intelligence

Byron York: What explains the FBI's deep faith in Trump dossier author Christopher Steele?

The FBI placed so much faith in Christopher Steele because he was a former British spy who had worked with the bureau a few years earlier in the world soccer corruption investigation. But there were problems with Steele's credibility, according to the referral. (Victoria Jones/PA via AP)

One of the most remarkable takeaways from the new documents released in the Trump-Russia investigation is the degree to which FBI officials were determined to believe dossier author Christopher Steele — even after it

(HPSCI) released his committee's memo on the FBI's use of the Steele dossier in surveillance requests to the Foreign Intelligence Surveillance Court regarding Trump campaign volunteer advisor Carter Page. Then Senators Grassley and Graham released on Feb. 6, a redacted version of their referral of Christopher Steele to the Department of Justice for criminal prosecution, which provided further details of FBI/DOJ fraud on the FISA Court. Graham and Grassley believe that Steele committed felonies by lying to the FBI about his media activities on behalf of the Clinton Campaign.

In using the dossier in the first application for surveillance of Page to the FISA court on Oct. 21, 2016, the FBI/DOJ officials, including James Comey and former Deputy Attorney General Sally Yates, relegated the fact that Steele's work had been entirely paid for by the Clinton Campaign and the DNC to a non-specific footnote referencing "political" origins. Although they were already in possession of a Yahoo!News article by their chief investigative correspondent Michael Isikoff specifically based on Steele's work, the FBI affirmed to the Court what Steele had apparently told them—that he only shared his work with Fusion GPS and the FBI, *not* the news media. This created the highly misleading impression that Isikoff's article validated Steele's allegations, which were otherwise uncorroborated. Moreover, Steele had already briefed the *Washington Post*, the *New York Times*, CNN, and the *New Yorker*, in addition to Isikoff, at the time of the Oct. 21, 2016 initial application. He had also briefed David Corn, Washing-

cc/MaynardClark

Sally Yates, former United States Deputy Attorney General under President Barack Obama.

ton Bureau Chief for *Mother Jones,* sometime in October.

According to the Graham/Grassley account, when Corn published his *Mother Jones* article on Oct. 31, it became clear to the FBI that Steele had lied to them about contacts with the news media. His informant status was terminated, but the FBI kept in contact with him through a back channel, very high up in the U.S. Department of Justice—Associate Deputy Attorney General Bruce Ohr. Ohr's wife, Nellie, worked for Steele's U.S. partner, Fusion GPS.

When the FBI/DOJ returned to the FISA Court in January 2017 to extend the Page surveillance, it engaged in yet another affirmative misrepresentation to the Court. While disclosing that Steele's informant relationship had been terminated because of his contacts with the news media, the DOJ/ FBI claimed to the Court that Steele only talked to the media in anger, when the Clinton email investigation was reopened and the Trump investigation seemed stalled. As Columnist Byron York notes in his excellent analysis for the *Washington Examiner*, the "whole Chris-was- angry-so-he-talked-to-the-press story was to allow the FBI to claim that his pre-anger work, i.e., the dossier, was credible." In the renewal application, the FBI again affirmatively asserted that it did not believe that Steele was the source of Isikoff's Sept. 23 article (which would, of course, call into question the *bona fides* of the entire application into question). Significantly, Steele confided to Bruce Ohr that he was extremely biased against Donald Trump and would do "anything" to prevent his election. This was never conveyed to the Court in the subsequent Page surveillance applications.

Fired former FBI Director Comey, who signed off

on the applications to the FISA Court, told the Congress in June 2017 that Steele's memos were "salacious and unverified." Yet the Nunes memo and Grassley/Graham referral make very clear that the dirty British work-product was used in an all-out effort to discredit candidate Trump, and now, to destroy his Presidency.

As whistleblower Bill Binney described it, the Nunes memo proves that the FBI knowingly used "paid propaganda" produced by one campaign "to go after another campaign" in their filing. Binney, a former top official in the National Security Agency, was targeted and persecuted by the FBI, and is therefore very familiar with their *modus operandi*.

It is not just this intelligence, released by Devin Nunes and Senators Grassley and Graham, which has produced howls of protest from the anti-Trumpers, from Rep. Adam Schiff, the Democratic leader of the House of Representatives Permanent Select Committee on Intelligence (HPSCI), and from media such as the *New York Times*, *Washington Post* and CNN. They, after all, were all part of the British operation against Trump, and now stand exposed and vulnerable. What they legitimately fear is that the Nunes memo represents what Binney called "a crack" which opens a view into the "corruption in the secret government."

In an attempt to cloak Steele with official immunities from what could be criminal prosecution, the *Washington Post*, on Feb. 7, insinuated that Steele was operating at the highest levels of official British intelligence when he concocted and spread his black propaganda memos against Donald Trump.

Nunes now says he is working on "Phase 2," which will examine the role of Obama State Department personnel in collaborating with Steele. One target of Nunes is Jonathan Winer, the Obama State Department's special envoy to Libya. Winer, a long-time number two to John Kerry, dating from Kerry's Senate days, is a significant anti-Putin legal fanatic who collaborated with Christopher Steele in the British-CIA/State Department coup in Ukraine. From 2014-2016, Steele wrote over 100 memos concerning Russia and Ukraine, which were provided to the case officer for the Ukraine coup, Victoria Nuland, then Assistant Secretary of State for European and Eurasian Affairs, as well as to Winer and Secretary of State John Kerry. In a speech to the U.S.-Ukraine Foundation, December 2013, Nuland had already stated that U.S. agencies spent over $5 billion to organize the illegal Ukraine coup, which employed neo-Nazis as military shock troops. Lifting the cover off this operation will not just shed light on the British role in orchestrat-

The then U.S. Secretary of State John Kerry (left) with Jonathan Winer (next to Kerry). Winer was Special Envoy to Libya, in Rome, Italy on Feb. 1, 2016.

ing an anti-Russian policy—destroying Ukraine in the process, while imposing punitive sanctions against Russia—but will also explain why the election of Trump caused so much hysteria in London and in Obama circles. He had pledged to end the "regime change" policies, such as that run against Ukraine, and instead to cooperate with Russia and Putin.

Steele also provided his dirty dossier on Trump to Nuland, Winer, and Kerry. In addition, two notorious Clinton operatives, Sidney Blumenthal and Cody Shearer, fed their dirt on Trump to Steele who, in turn, fed it to the FBI.

MI-6, the FBI and the Dodgy Dossier

One sign of involvement of the highest levels of British intelligence was the deployment this week of a Foreign Office attorney to a London High Court hearing, where a deposition of Steele was to be held. Steele is being sued by Russian businessman Aleksej Gubarev, who is accused by Steele of "hacking" Democratic Party emails during the campaign, supposedly on behalf of the Kremlin. Steele did not show for the deposition, but his lawyer argued that he should not be forced to testify, as the deposition might "require the disclosure of sensitive information which could endanger UK national security interests and personnel." The Foreign Office attorney was present to make sure that such "sensitive information" was not disclosed!

Another sign of British intelligence involvement was a revealing article about Steele in the Feb. 7 *Washington Post*, titled "Hero or Hired Gun? How a Former British Spy Became a Flashpoint in the Russia Investigation." Even though it is one of the leaders in the anti-Trump campaign, the *Post* revealed that Steele was guided by the former chief of MI-6, Sir Richard Dearlove, who headed MI-6 from 1999 to 2004. The article states that Dearlove and a former British Ambassador to Moscow and associate of Steele, Sir Andrew Wood, steered Steele to the FBI.

According to the story, Steele and his partner at Sterling Select Partners, LLC, Chris Burrows, went to Dearlove "for guidance," as they claimed to be "rattled" by what they were discovering about Trump and Russia while compiling their "dodgy dossier." It was Dearlove who was responsible for an earlier "dodgy dossier"— that is, the lying report on Iraq's "weapons of mass destruction," which was used by then-Prime Minister Tony Blair to bolster arguments, in collaboration with George W. Bush, Dick Cheney and the neocon unilateralists, for launching the second Iraq war, a war which toppled Saddam Hussein, devastated Iraq, and led to the creation of ISIS. Dearlove said "he advised Steele and Burrows to work discreetly with a top British government official to pass along information to the FBI." He praised Steele, whose expertise he described as "superb."

One striking omission in the *Post*'s article was its failure to mention the role of Robert Hannigan in launching the targeting of Trump and Putin. The British have previously and proudly claimed this role. Hannigan was the Director of the Government Communications Headquarters (GCHQ), the British snooping agency, which the *Guardian* described as the "principle whistleblower" of the Russia-Trump connection, a connection the GCHQ allegedly "discovered" in the summer of 2015. According to the British account, Hannigan personally passed the evidence compiled by the GCHQ to CIA Director John Brennan in June 2016. It was then that Brennan launched a "major inter-agency investigation," which included the FBI and the Director

of National Intelligence, James Clapper.

Steele's first memo was completed June 20, 2016, and his first meeting with an FBI official was July 5, just weeks before Trump received the Republican Party's nomination.

Thus, before Obama's intelligence *apparat* of Comey, CIA Director Brennan and Director of National Intelligence Clapper declared Jan. 6, 2017 that there was unassailable evidence that Russia meddled in the election, and that Trump colluded with the Russians, it was GCHQ which initiated the fake narrative of Russiagate. This was to be used as an "insurance policy," should Trump win, as admitted in a text message to his FBI attorney mistress, Lisa Page, by FBI operative Peter Strzok, chief of Counterintelligence who was part of the inter-agency investigation.

Threats to Trump as Russiagate Implodes

The British were reacting to Trump's pledge to find ways to work with Putin, rather than to demonize and provoke him, as was Obama Administration policy. Such a prospect represented an existential threat to the imperial, geopolitical doctrine of a unilateral world order, under London/Wall Street control. The hundreds of pages of text messages sent between Peter Strzok and Lisa Page provide a glimpse of this hysteria, as the two wrote about the plotting against Trump going on in "Andy's office," a reference to the former Deputy Director of the FBI, Andrew McCabe.

Strzok described himself as "riled up" over the possibility that Trump might win, referring to him as "a f**king idiot.... What the f**k happened to our country?" Page responded by describing Trump as a "loathsome human being." Both worked for a while on spe-

Philip Mudd, former CIA officer and FBI official.

cial counsel Robert Mueller's team, until the Justice Department's Inspector General released the texts, and Strzok was removed. He also played a lead role in the investigation of Hillary Clinton's violation of national security by her use of an unsecured private email server when she was Secretary of State. Hillary Clinton was eventually given a slap on the wrist, with Strzok advising Comey to weaken the language in his finding, so as to avoid the possibility of a felony charge against her. During this period, Strzok admitted to Page that they had found "no there there" in the Trump investigation—meaning that no evidence exists to back the charges of meddling and collusion!

As the story of Russiagate falls apart, defenders of the FBI and CIA are resorting to blatant threats against the President. Philip Mudd, a former CIA officer whom Robert Mueller personally moved to the FBI to supervise Mueller's huge informant program, told CNN in August 2017 that "this government is going to kill this guy," referring to President Trump. Mudd, now a CNN consultant, lashed out Feb. 2 against the Nunes memo on CNN. Parroting the argument of Congressional Democrats about the memo, he said it is an attack on the FBI's "ability to conduct an investigation with integrity.... The FBI people are ticked... You think you can intimidate the director? You better think again, Mr. President." He added, "I know how the game is played. We're going to win."

CNN host Wolf Blitzer responded, "You don't want the FBI angry at you," whereupon Gloria Borger, CNN's chief political analyst, blurted out, "Trump is playing a dangerous game." It should be noted that CNN just hired Josh Campbell, a former top aide to Comey, to join its team, while NBC-TV hired John Brennan to provide "commentary."

Not to be outdone, the *Washington Post* ran an op-ed by Eugene Robinson Feb. 5, titled "Trump has Picked a Fight with the FBI. He'll be Sorry." Referring to the sordid history of the FBI persecution of Rev. Martin Luther King, Jr., who was a target for harassment and threats from the FBI from the mid-1950s until his assassination in 1968, Robinson warns, "Presidents don't win fights with the FBI. He'll be sorry." While the FBI and the CIA were involved in the coverup of the assassinations of both President John F. Kennedy and King, Lyndon LaRouche has reported on the role of the British as the authors of key assassinations in U.S. history, including the murders of Alexander Hamilton, Abraham Lincoln, William McKinley, Kennedy, and King.

Which brings us finally back to the British role in Russiagate, and the prophetic insights of the LaRouches. In the Jan. 20, 2017 *EIR* on the day of Trump's inauguration, Helga Zepp LaRouche wrote, "What is spectacular about the operation against Trump, however, is that British intelligence and its American counterparts, which have operated for decades as spooks in the shadows, have now been forced to expose themselves openly. The essentially dilettantish operation—conducted by Steele, the man in charge of exposing the corruption in The Federation International de Football Association (FIFA) and the principal MI-6 agent in the affair of former officer of the Russian FSB secret service, Alexander Litvinenko's murder (whose death he and the Brits blame on Putin's FSB operatives)—revealed the direct intervention of the British empire, for which the term 'globalization' is only a synonym, into the internal affairs of the United States."

In April 2017, as it was becoming clear that the anti-Trumpers intended to remove Trump through impeachment, the 25th Amendment, or even murder, Lyndon LaRouche stated that "No British institution has the right to meddle in American affairs. Obama is an example of this evil. Mankind has to learn to fight, to shut down things that are wrong. The British empire is wrong.... People must have the guts to do what must be done. The time has come to crush this thing. Get this nation and other nations to agree to that."

The revelations during the last weeks, of the British role behind the regime-change operation in the United States, demonstrate that there are some who are finally showing "the guts to do what must be done."

In the Midst of a Profound Political Realignment— Our Task Is To Consolidate It

by Bill Roberts

Feb. 13—As of this writing, both the world and the United States are in the process of a profound political realignment, the reality of which is not necessarily obvious, but is, nevertheless, right in front of our noses. An international shift of nations away from the sphere of influence of British empire geopolitics, toward a cooperative relationship with those nations participating with China in the Belt and Road Initiative, is dramatic and irreversible at this point. This new paradigm of cooperative development, spearheaded in recent years by China's President Xi Jinping, is already transforming the world, and it poses the only positive alternative to the increasing danger posed to mankind by the declining influence and stability of the outgoing British model of global empire.

There is also another, related political realignment taking place. It is indicated by the electoral shift that propelled Donald Trump into the Presidency, especially centered in the mid-western states of America, where Trump performed far better than previous "Republican" presidential candidates. It involves formerly productively-employed workers and farmers who once represented a fairly loyal base of Democratic Party voters in such states as Michigan, Iowa, Wisconsin and upstate New York, where counties and precincts that voted once or twice for Obama gave their vote to Donald Trump. In some of these areas, for example in certain Detroit blue collar suburbs, many voters split their vote, chosing Trump at the top of the ticket, but local Democrats in down-ticket races. If one looks at a map of the 2008 Presidential election in Michigan, the areas that voted Democratic versus Republican, we see a patchwork quilt: the northern part of Michigan, the Upper Peninsula, tended to be Democratic up until 2008; many rural areas and small working class towns across the state often leaned Democratic. Fast forward to 2016, and we see that this phenomenon hardly exists any longer. Virtually all of these counties supported the election of Trump, and a similar story exists across our industrial heartland.

In these recent developments we are seeing shades of 1986, when, in a statewide Illinois election, the LaRouche political movement shocked the entire political establishment, electing candidates to statewide positions in the Democratic primary. That 1986 vote was a similar phenomenon to what we are seeing today, with disenfranchised, formerly productive workers, rural voters, and a significant portion of the black population of Chicago turning out to vote against the Democratic Party establishment.

The similarity to today? In both 1986 and 2016, people kept turning on the television and hearing endless news reports about the great economic recovery, a supposed recovery which bore no resemblance to the reality of the steadily worsening condition of their own lives. Voters knew they were being lied to, and they wanted someone who was going to stick it to those guys in Washington.

Take the case today of Appalachia, in the coal country of West Virginia and Eastern Kentucky. These were the areas visited by Robert Kennedy in 1968, weeks before he announced his bid for President, areas that remained loyally Democratic for thirty years after that tour. Kennedy, himself the heir to a great fortune, nevertheless found in the people of Appalachia, as in the Mississippi Delta, those whose extreme poverty required the attention and authority of the federal government to transform their situation. Kennedy's appeal to their humanity, for the necessity to unleash the capacities of that region for the benefit of the whole nation, was not soon forgotten by those downtrodden men and women.

Today, no state in the union supports President

Trump more than West Virginia, the heart of Appalachia. Not only did Trump win every single county in the state, but, as of this month, 61% of West Virginians approve of Trump's job as President. While Trump campaigned in West Virginia on bringing back coal jobs and tackling the opioid crisis ravaging the state—these are not the areas where the people of West Virginia have so far seen the greatest success in the policies of Donald J. Trump during his first year in office. It was in the midst of Trump's state visit to China, that the China Energy Investment Corporation announced their intention to invest $84 billion in West Virginia, to put the people of West Virginia to work not in raw material extraction, but in the manufacture of value-added chemical products that will be sold back to China, to the U.S.A. and worldwide. As Governor Jim Justice pointed out, this makes all the difference in the world for a state that had a projected $500 million shortfall going into the 2018 fiscal budget.

Fulfilling the Election Mandate

This West Virginia breakthrough, part of a $254 billion investment package from Chinese companies, stands in stark contrast to the ongoing fierce pressure being applied against President Trump by the institutional financial and political power of London and Wall Street, to prevent him from carrying out the in-depth rebuilding of the nation's infrastructure which he wants. The recently released infrastructure plan, written by Wall Street insiders, is a non-starter. It calls for only $200 billion in federal funds, with the other $800 billion to come from states and public-private partnerships. It is a not-so-thinly veiled plan to coerce individual states to enter into PPPs, which will be dominated by financial speculators for their own benefit, as well as to submit to the privatizations of already existing state-owned infrastructure. The striking irony is that Trump was able to secure a larger sum of investment from China than the federal expenditure proposed by this Goldman Sachs-authored plan.

It is not by propping up a Wall Street bubble that we will secure the future for the nation, but in unleashing the productive powers of labor inherent in our highly-skilled workforce. It was this desire, and this perceived possibility that drove the political realignment seen in the 2016 election. Donald Trump did not campaign either as a Republican or a Democrat, a conservative or a moderate, but as a builder, as someone who intends to get things done, to reverse the trend of destruction of our industrial workforce, to recommit to the mission of building a future.

It is that future which most Americans want, and in the minds of the national electorate, party labels now mean nothing—except to the blind inhabitants of the inside-the-beltway Washington, D.C. madhouse, who squat, pondering which end of the egg to crack open.

In the real world, local elected officials, small businessmen, and farmers, and organized blocks of constituents spread among the cities and counties of our nation, now have a profound power to shape the economic policy of the country, away from the grip of Wall Street. In other words, we have in our hands a dramatic political realignment, whose character—although ignored by media pundits—was irrefutably given existence in the 2016 election. That realignment is well underway, but it is not yet consolidated enough to be able to push through the necessary policy solutions. That fight defines our immediate mission.

Outside of the borders of the United States, the global realignment among nations is proceeding apace. Railroads are being built. Dams and hydro-electric projects are being built. Nuclear power plants are being built. Land is being reclaimed and developed for agriculture. Longevity is increasing, and the conditions of life for hundreds of millions of people are improving. Nation after nation is joining in the China-initiated Belt and Road global development project. The natural next step for a politically realigned United States is to wholeheartedly enlist in this win-win perspective.

This points to what should be the obvious. Under our own Federal Constitution, as adopted in 1788 and then put into practice under George Washington, it falls to the federal government—both in its Constitutional role and as a sacred responsibility—to generate large sums of credit for public projects—to build the nation. This is easily accomplished by creating Credit Banks based on the Alexander Hamilton model. Private financial speculators and sharks have no role to play in the arena of national Public Credit. Ironically, it is China which adopted this "American" approach since no later than the early 1990s. The political realignment now occurring—both globally and within the United States—demands just such a Hamiltonian approach by all the principals involved. It is that approach which is scientifically defined by Lyndon LaRouche in his Four New Laws of June 13, 2014. Those Four Laws, as elaborated by LaRouche, define both the solution to the current crisis, as well as the basis for a consolidation of the political realignment now underway within the United States. This is the way to build the future.

The Hong Kong-Zhuhai-Macao Bridge—For China and the World

by Michael Billington

Feb. 11—On July 1, 2018, barring unforeseen obstacles, the world's longest bridge, including the world's longest underwater road tunnel, will be officially opened for traffic. It should be no surprise that this engineering feat is taking place in China, where most of the world's new records are being set over the past decade. This 55 km bridge-tunnel connects the former British colony of Hong Kong to the former Portuguese colony of Macao and the neighboring Chinese metropolis of Zhuhai, crossing over the open sea at the mouth of the Pearl River, called the Lingdingyang channel.

Xinhua/Liang Xu

Aerial photo of the Hong Kong-Zhuhai-Macao Bridge on Dec. 27, 2017.

In the beautifully produced two-part documentary on China's CGTN, titled "Hong Kong-Zhuhai-Macao Bridge," Peter Wu, the Vice President of China Construction America (a subsidiary of the world's largest construction company, China State Construction Engineering), speaking in New York City, says:

"New York City became what it is today because of these bridges. From the late 1900s to 1950, your civil engineers created a lot of miracles—including the Brooklyn Bridge, the George Washington Bridge, Lincoln Tunnel, Holland Tunnel, Grand Central Terminal, JFK Airport—and the whole world still benefits from those engineering innovations."

Meng Fanchao, the Chief Engineer for the Hong Kong-Zhuhai-Macao (HKZM) Bridge, then adds:

"Prior to the 1970s, where was the global center of bridge building? In Europe and America. From the 1970s to the early 21st Century, where was this center? In Japan. The Japanese, after their economy took off, built some of the worlds greatest cross-sea bridges and tunnels. Since the early 21st Century, you could say this center is in China."

The Birth of a Great Project

The first proposal for the project came from Gordon Wu, the founder of the huge Hong Kong conglomerate Hopewell Holdings, in 1983. Soon after the historic return of Hong Kong sovereignty to China in 1997, Beijing offered its support to the project, and in 2003 Hong Kong's Chief Secretary Donald Tsang went to Beijing to set in motion the "HKZM Bridge Advance Work Coordination Group." In 2008, the central and local governments agreed to finance 42% of the costs, with the remainder to be a loan from the Bank of China

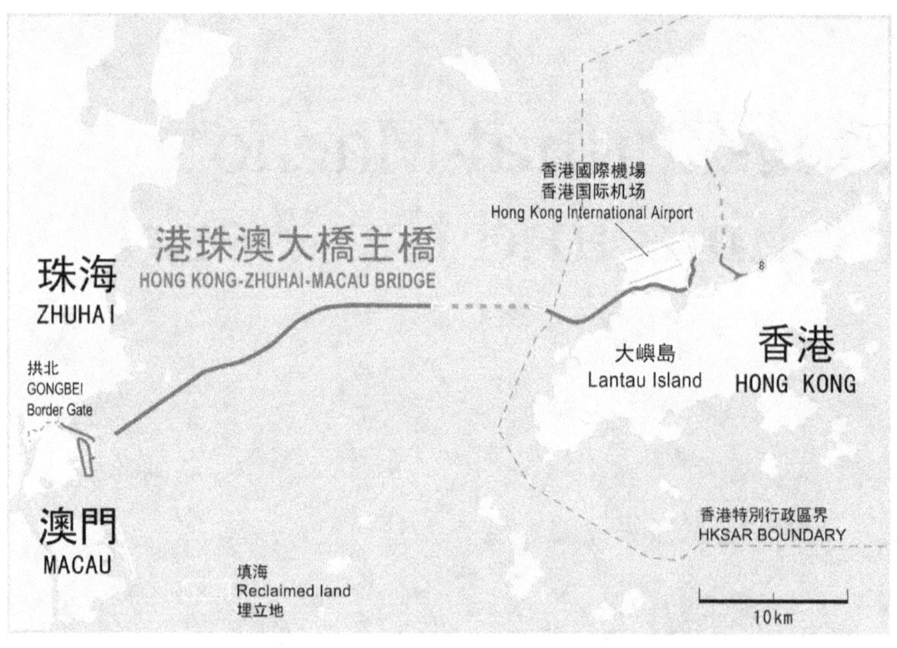

Diagram showing the bridge-tunnel complex which connects the former British- and Portuguese-owned cities, Hong Kong and Macau, to China.

(this was later revised to 22% from the governments and 78% in loans from a consortium of banks, headed by Bank of China).

Construction began in 2009, with a target completion of date of 2016—but environmentalists, led by London's World Wildlife Fund (WWF), protested, holding up the process. The WWF issued a report in 2009 titled "The Hong Kong-Zhuhai-Macao Bridge is a Dangerous Experiment on Chinese White Dolphins." The CGTN documentary discusses the measures taken in response, even including limiting noise in the construction process. This and other unforeseen problems delayed the original timetable, but nonetheless the completion of this astonishing project in less than a decade is a major achievement.

The project not only provides a physical connection between the former European colonial outposts of Hong Kong and Macao, but it has reunited the people of these former colonies to the mainland Chinese people in a way not seen before. Beijing's official relationship with these former colonies, called "One Country, Two Systems," is based on a considerable degree of local governmental control in Hong Kong and Macao, with the understanding that the economic and cultural differences would only be melded together over time. The thousands of engineers and skilled laborers who have built the bridge came from all over China, working to achieve a common goal, to enhance the tremendous productivity of the Pearl River Estuary region, which already produces 10% of the nation's productive output.

Su Quanke, the chief engineer on the project, says in the CGTV documentary: "We've built a connection, a link. It's more than just a physical link. It connects our thoughts, our sentiments, and the good things we have created together over the years. It has linked our technological standards, our regulations, and our thinking." Chief Designer Meng Fanchao says that the bridge "also had a symbolic meaning—a clear focus on the aesthetics of bridge-building culture. Anyone who sees it will likely agree—this is more than a man-made structure, it's a cultural vehicle."

Schiller Institute Chairwoman Helga Zepp-LaRouche, known in China as the Silk Road Lady, visited the nearly completed bridge in November 2017, after speaking at a Zhuhai forum on the 21st Century Maritime Silk Road. Describing the experience after her return to Germany, she said:

"For me, the absolute high point was traveling over the new sea bridge. It is really a total masterpiece of engineering. They had to invent 120 new patented techniques to build this bridge. For example, it has tunnels and artificial islands, and some of the underground area is very soft, so they had to develop new techniques to drive cylinders into the ground. It was just incredible. It took them only eight years to build this unbelievable, very, very beautiful and modern bridge. And if you compare that, for example, with the abysmally slow speed at which even reconstruction of highways is being done in Germany or elsewhere, it really shows that the New Silk Road Spirit and the idea of the Chinese economic miracle—you know, it is something which used to be German, which used to be the German economic miracle, but people here have forgotten that. I think we need a completely new view on how we build things, on how we reconstruct our infrastructure. Really, we can learn a lot from the Chinese right now."

The statistics are indeed incredible. The main bridge section is 22.9 kilometers long, with three cable-stayed spans at the highest point, between 280 and 460 meters in length. The original plan was for a bridge to cover the full length, which would have required an 80 meter-high bridge, with 200 meter towers, in order to allow the 4,000 or more ships that pass through the estuary each day to clear the bridge. However, Hong Kong International Airport, which is close to the HKZM bridge, restricts nearby buildings to a height limit of 88 meters for reasons of safety for aircraft. This required the addition of the 6.7 km undersea tunnel, which was not only an unprecedented engineering feat, but also required the building of two artificial islands at either end of the tunnel.

Due to the soft seabed, this required the innovation of driving 120 huge steel cylinders into the seabed, forming an oval perimeter for the artificial islands. Each cylinder is 22.5 meters in diameter, 55 meters high, and weighs 550 tons. The cylinders were fabricated in Shanghai, each one requiring 72 pieces welded together—12,960 6-ton steel plates were used altogether.

An excellent PowerPoint presentation on this process, and all the technical aspects of the construction of the bridge, was given by Albert T. Young of the Department of Engineering at the University of Hong Kong on Nov. 23, 2017.

The Chinese Dream

The closing of the CGTN Documentary is quite poetic, capturing the historic nature of this grand project:

"Bridges overcome barriers. Throughout history, they have brought people closer together. The HKZM Bridge connects the Chinese mainland to Hong Kong and Macao. It also connects China to the world.

"But this bridge does more than connect regions—it connects China's past, its present, and its future. After almost 70 years of development, China has grown from a fledgling that had only just learned to fly, to a great bird, spreading its wings and souring into the sky. The concepts of Chinese standards and 'Made in China' are increasingly making their impact felt on the world stage. As for the HKZM Bridge, it's the latest, most impressive symbol of the Chinese Dream."

To Solve Cape Town's Water Crisis, Bring in Russia, China, And U.S.A. To Help

by Ramasimong Phillip Tsokolibane

Feb. 10—The City of Cape Town, with a population of more than 4 million, and several surrounding provinces, are facing a hundred-year drought and an unprecedented water crisis. Water use restrictions have become increasingly severe over the past weeks and months. The City now says it will "turn off the taps" on May 11. On Feb. 6, R.P. Tsokolibane, leader of LaRouche South Africa, published the following statement on the necessary international *response to the crisis. His statement was promptly acknowledged by the City, which noted that it "will be sent to the relevant Task Team for consideration." The national government announced on Feb. 8 that a cabinet task team has been formed in Pretoria, and that the necessary steps are being taken to declare, within days, that the drought is a national disaster. This crisis follows years of obstruction by the British imperial interest that is hostile to population growth, including environmentalist operations—operations that are continuing even now.*

Sometimes it is necessary to state clearly some very simple things. Such is the case with the fresh water crisis that threatens the citizens of our second greatest city, Cape Town.

As the South African leader of the international movement of the American physical economist and statesman, Lyndon LaRouche, let me say it loud and clear:

No matter the circumstance which has brought us to this point, it is totally unacceptable to let the crisis go on to the point that Cape Town's water pipes are depressurised by turning off the taps, or by running dry—on May 11 or on any date.

Turn off the taps and the waterborne sewage system will back up. You can't flush! In a city, that means cholera. Depressurising the freshwater pipes permits inleaking of waterborne, disease-causing organisms, and again, people will die, mainly from diarrheal diseases. Depressurising and repressurising the pipes also causes main breaks, especially in older pipes. For water engineers and public health experts, this is standard, textbook stuff.

Forget all the finger pointing and blame shaming; there are many, who through their fantasies, inaction,

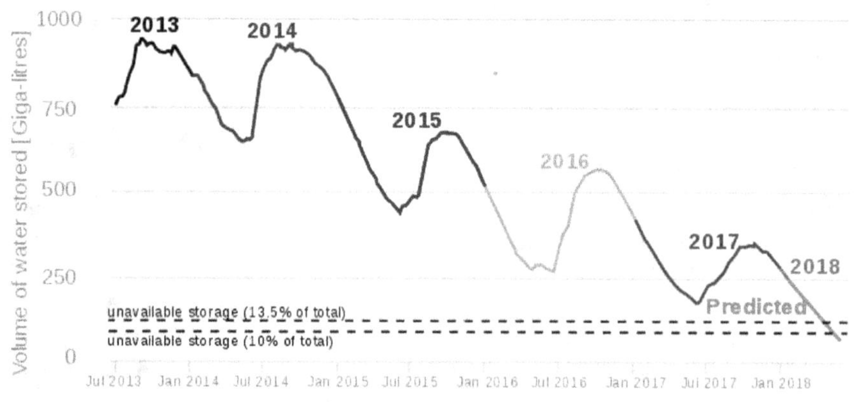

Graph of the total water stored in the Western Cape's largest six dams from June 30, 2013 to Jan. 15, 2018. The graph illustrates the declining water storage levels over the course of the Cape Town water crisis. Data obtained from the Climate Systems Analysis Group.

or outright stupidity, would need to be held accountable for letting the crisis get to this extreme moment. But assessing blame and holding people accountable, will not get fresh water to the people of Cape Town, either now or in the future.

In determining what to do, we start with the obvious: In an area prone to drought with cyclical certainty, we cannot rely on Mother Nature alone to provide the needed fresh water, especially if we want that area to grow and prosper. Until now, some may have thought it cheaper in the short term to get by with erratic rainfall, but we are now finding out that such an approach may have seemed pennywise, but is most assuredly pound foolish.

U.S. Navy photo/Photographer's Mate 2nd Class Prince A. Hughes III
Potential emergency water source: The Nimitz-class aircraft carrier USS Carl Vinson, capable of desalinating 400,000 gallons of potable water daily, is shown in San Diego, Calif.

Therefore, we must provide the necessary credit to move freshwater from where it is plentiful, to Cape Town and its environs, and at the same time develop new, human-created sources of fresh water such as offshore nuclear-powered desalination plants, which also hold prospect of providing additional electrical power. Through the vision of our present national government and its leadership, we now have the potential to fund such systems through credits issued by the African branch of the BRICS' New Development Bank in Johannesburg, so that the systems are put in place and functioning as rapidly as possible.

Simultaneously, we should also develop large-scale water recycling and waste management systems, using available advanced technologies, to make grey water reusable for human and industrial consumption.

But we must also come up with an emergency plan to bring new fresh water to Cape Town, to bridge the gap until these new systems come on line, and when, also, the region might once again happily receive sufficient rain to replenish dry reservoirs.

I would strongly urge that, having admitted the seriousness of the problem, we bring not only our own forces and cadre to bear, but also international reinforcements. I would call on our BRICS friends in both Russia and China, who have extensive experience in these matters, as I would also call on U.S. President Trump to send qualified people to help, as well as the Israelis, who are experts in such water management matters. Let us do this quickly, so that we can bring to bear all the forces needed. Let us do this immediately!

For example, the modern aircraft carriers of the major powers have the capability of desalinating large amounts of water beyond the requirements of their crews.

Some of these programmes are already being implemented as part of the City of Cape Town's Emergency Water Augmentation Scheme, including the construction of temporary desalination plants and the bringing up of ground water by means of bore holes, but it is generally acknowledged that none of these measures, including the restrictions which have already reduced Cape Town's consumption by one half, will be sufficient or be delivered in time to avoid Day Zero. Additional measures should be taken.

We need a thorough evaluation of the state of all of our national infrastructure, with a view to its improvement. The people of Cape Town are the victims of short-term, wishful thinking, when what has been needed all along is to work from a long-term plan based on science and human creativity, to solve eminently solvable problems. Let us learn, now, this important lesson.

I, and the international movement I represent in South Africa, stand ready to help in this process.

POET-MATHEMATICIAN SERIES, PART IV

Sophie Germain

by David Shavin

Feb. 9—China has put on the table the beautiful—and very "American"—mission of wiping out poverty in China by the year 2020. The type of thinking required today to finally wipe out poverty, disease and hunger will involve a level of creativity once described by Lyndon LaRouche as being able to "play ping-pong with the stars." The beautiful composition of a new alliance of nations—pushing the frontiers of plasma physics, fusion technologies, and materials processing, as the economic surplus is deployed to craft massive infrastructure projects throughout the developing world—requires a level of thinking and emotional development that will make future generations stand in awe. This type of thinking is that of the "poet-mathematician." It was also expressed in Plato's Re-public as that of the "philosopher-king"—the almost impossible, but completely necessary development of leaders, who pursue the most difficult paradoxes in astronomy and music, so as to harmonize their souls with the complexities of the

Sophie Germain

development of human communities. After the American Revolution, a youthful genius, Karl Gauss, in what was apparently an obscure mathematical text, went boldly where most others feared to tread. An identifiable, small core of youth, took up Gauss's challenge while he was alive. They were Sophie Germain, Lejeune Dirichlet, Niels Abel, Evariste Galois and Bernhard Riemann.

Lawfully, and somewhat ironically, the individuals who most seriously, most passionately, took up this mission, have proven to be, as rather unique individuals, the most fascinating exemplars, in their own personalities, of the higher-ordered mathematics. The historically-specific realities of their lives rise to a level beyond mere biographical side-notes—a level helpful in delineating how they were able to develop such a rigorous and higher-ordered language, appropriate for mapping how the mind intervenes upon the outside world.

The case of Sophie Germain closes this series on Gauss's five prime students, all poet-mathematicians.[1]

Though not well-appreciated, Sophie Germain was the first serious student of Gauss's *Disquisitiones Arithmeticae*, or *DA*. Even less appreciated is that her work with Gauss served her as the uniquely appropriate "aesthetic education" for her probe of unseen harmonies of music. Again, as with Dirichlet, Abel, Galois and Riemann, we shall find a non-'mathematical', musical core that guided her work in both science and art. And, again, the historically-specific moral core of Sophie Germain's too-lonely battle

---

1. The case for Dirichlet was made here: http://www.larouchepub.com/other/2010/3723rebecca_dirichlet.html The other three are listed as Parts I to III, and found at: I. Abel. II. Galois. III. Riemann.

for beauty and truth is identifiable, and it was the driving force of her accomplishments.

Sophie Germain recognized the need for the poet-mathematician. She wrote that decent leaders in normal times may be clever enough. "In times of crisis, however, it's something else. Circumstances become pressing; we must know how to make prompt decisions; we also often need courage, and courage is not necessarily a quality of the clever man." Germain will make the case for the unity of courage and genius, that it requires the mastering of the modalities of Karl Friedrich Gauss—and, perhaps surprisingly, the modalities of J.S. Bach.

Carl Gauss

I. Archimedes and Gauss

In the three years after Gauss's 1801 *DA*, Germain launched into an intensive study of the work. In 1804, she first wrote to Gauss, developing some further implications of his work. She began, "Monsieur—For a long time your *Disquisitiones Arithmeticae* has been an object of my admiration and study." In her letter, she developed a subsection of Gauss's "4n+3" primes, now called "Germain primes," to develop an approach to proving Fermat's last theorem. She signed the letter "Monsieur LeBlanc," as she feared she would not be taken seriously if the name on the letter were that of a woman.[2] Gauss wrote LeBlanc, pleased that he had taken up "the research to which he [Gauss] devoted the most beautiful part of his youth…" After the third letter from "LeBlanc," Gauss told Heinrich Olbers, his astro-

nomical collaborator: "I am amazed that M. LeBlanc has completely mastered my Disq. Arith., and has sent me very respectable communications about them."

When in 1807, Gauss discovered that his correspondent was actually a woman, one Sophie Germain, he was more than delighted:

"But how to describe to you my admiration and astonishment at seeing my esteemed correspondent Monsieur Le Blanc metamorphose himself into this illustrious personage who gives such a brilliant example of what I would find it difficult to believe. A taste for the abstract sciences in general and above all the mysteries of numbers is excessively rare. One is not astonished at it—the enchanting charms of this sublime science reveal only to those who have the courage to go deeply into it. But when a person of the sex which, according to our customs and prejudices, must encounter infinitely more difficulties than men to familiarize herself with these thorny researches, succeeds nevertheless in surmounting these obstacles and penetrating the most obscure parts of them, then without doubt she must have the noblest courage, quite extraordinary talents and superior genius. Indeed nothing could prove to me in so flattering and less equivocal manner that the attractions of this science, which has enriched my life with so many joys, are not chimerical, as the predilection with which you have honored it."

But even more telling was the story behind the revelation of her identity. During Napoleon's 1806 invasion of Germany, Germain had requested a family friend, General Joseph-Marie Pernety, to intervene, and to extend protection to Gauss. When Gauss was told that his protectress was one Sophie Germain, he was puzzled, saying that the only woman that he was acquainted with in Paris was the wife of an astronomer-friend, and not anyone named "Sophie Germain." The general reported this back to Germain, and she wrote to Gauss, explaining that, in fact, he did know her, that she was his correspondent, M. LeBlanc. That occasioned

---

2. As part of her disguise, Germain instructed Gauss that he could write back to "LeBlanc" at the address of one Silvestre de Sacy. This was a family friend, Antoine Isaac, Baron Silvestre de Sacy, a linguist from a Jewish family of Paris. Of some note, while Germain was decoding Gauss's *DA*, the linguist was working on the decoding of the famous Rosetta Stone. (Later, de Sacy personally initiated both Champollion and Thomas Young into the project.)

Gauss's letter (above). However, what she didn't explain to Gauss was the psychological horror behind her actions. For her, Gauss represented the precious, rare mind of an Archimedes; and she was horrified that Gauss might receive the same treatment as Archimedes had—murdered by an occupying force.

The key, formative and driving experience for Germain was when, as a thirteen-year-old, the turbulence, confusion and violence of the 1789 revolution sent the sensitive Sophie into her father's library, where she delved into Montaclu's *Histoire des Mathematiques*.[3] There, amidst the stories of scientific investigations and discoveries over thousands of years, Sophie made an intimate friend of the great mind of Archimedes. But she learned, to her horror, that such a treasured man, in the midst of his intellectual concentration, was struck down by a Roman soldier. There, the inspiring and beautiful pursuit of truth was confronted with the brutally senseless. During the senseless horrors of the next five years in Paris, culminating in the infamous "Terror," the sensitive teenager pursued her struggle for eternal verities.

From that point on, Sophie kept her bond with Archimedes. Despite familial and social pressures to adopt a more traditional position for a woman, and with no hope of a professional career, Sophie pursued her mission. Five years later, at eighteen, Sophie took advantage of the availability of lecture notes from the presentations at the newly-founded Ecole Polytechnique. She submitted responses to them under the name of "M. LeBlanc," at that time, the name of an actual student at the Ecole. When the professor, Joseph Lagrange, wanted to meet this Antoine-August LeBlanc, the student with such apt observations, Germain's identity was disclosed. Over the next ten years, various professors would treat the young woman as a talented oddity, the woman-mathematician. Typically, they would offer their own textbooks to her as the proper next step for her self-improvement. Germain was not excited about playing the role of Eliza Doolittle for Professor Higgins, and she avoided such attentions.

Prior to Gauss, it would appear that only Adrien-Marie Legendre took her mind seriously enough to

answer questions and engage in dialogue.[4] The revelation in 1807, that Monsieur LeBlanc was actually Sophie Germain, appears to have actually increased Gauss's interest level in his correspondent's character and mental powers. For the first time in three years of correspondence, Gauss described to her three new theorems on cubic and biquadratic residues; however, he deliberately omitted his proofs, as he explained, "...in order not to deprive you of the pleasure of finding them yourself, if you find it worthy of your time... Continue, Mademoiselle, to favor me with your friendship and your correspondence, which are my pride, and be persuaded that I am and will always be with the highest esteem, Your most sincere admirer."

Two months later, Gauss received his three proofs. Germain wrote, "How I have enjoyed reading your three theorems on residues! I have searched for demonstrations of them. I add them to my letter in order to have you judge them.... In attempting to provide proofs for them, I have developed a way of thinking that for me is full of charm."

II. Classical—'A Way of Thinking That for Me Is Full of Charm'

The strategic role of Gauss in this series involves his complete development of Johannes Kepler. Kepler had taken up the challenge in Plato's *Timaeus* and developed the incredible but true, underlying coherence between such "objective" matters as the organization of the solar system and such "subjective" matters as the harmonic ordering of the mind's hearing. The planets were organized just as the human ear heard musical intervals. Now, this is, indeed, what puts the "classical" in classical. The core of the human identity, the mind, is uniquely tuned to be in synch with the most powerful forces in creation, and so to be capable of bringing them under deliberate mastery. A world lacking this characteristic simply would not be classical.

Gauss relentlessly pushed forward this classical double-counterpoint of Kepler. At the same time that Gauss composed his *DA* on the unseen harmonies of the human mind, he also shocked European scientists by showing how Kepler's approach solved the seem-

---

3. In 1789, her father, Ambroise-François Germain, was elected deputy of the Third Estate for the city of Paris, and was a member of the National Assembly at Versailles. (Apparently, he took public positions against "agiotage," that is, making a business out of currency exchange.) Later, in 1800, he would become a Directeur of the Banque de France.

4. Legendre's 1798 "*Essai sur la théorie des nombres*" impressed Germain. It probably led Germain to Gauss's 1801 work, where she would find both corrections of Legendre and a much fuller development.

ingly unsolvable "objective" problem of the orbit of Ceres.[5] It might be surprising to some, but his *DA* of 1801 is best understood as an intensive exploration and development of the geography of the inner workings of the human mind. How else to understand the miracle of the reciprocity of two different species of prime numbers?

Though Sophie Germain certainly had studied Gauss more than anyone else, she had also read her Kepler. And, as of her completion of the three proofs for Gauss in 1807, she had developed this way of thinking, one that she found "full of charm." It would lead to her winning the scientific prize of the French Academy for her work on the underlying patterns of sound.

5. Jonathan Tennenbaum and Bruce Director, "How Gauss Determined the Orbit of Ceres" https://www.schillerinstitute.org/fid_97-01/982_orbit_ceres.pdf

---

Quadratic Reciprocity and Political Revolutions

The harmonic patterns in Gauss's residues are no less fascinating than the beautiful Chladni patterns.

Gauss examined how numbers had something in common if they shared the same modulus—that is, if divided by the same number, they yielded the same remainder, or residue. So, 11 and 18 both yield 4 with respect to the modulus 7. Next, Gauss compared the quadratic series—the squares of 1, 2, 3…, that is, 1, 4, 9…—in terms of a given prime-number modulus. Four examples may assist:

Squares	1	4	9	16	25	36	49	64	81	100	121	144	169	196	225	256
Mod 7	1	4	2	2	4	1	0	1	4	2	2	4	1	0	1	4
Mod 11	1	4	9	5	3	3	5	9	4	1	0	1	4	9	5	3
Mod 13	1	4	9	3	12	10	10	12	3	9	4	1	0	1	4	9
Mod 17	1	4	9	16	8	2	15	13	13	15	2	8	16	9	4	1

Gauss found that every modulus displayed patterns as to how their quadratic residues spread out. First, for a modulus of size n, all the numbers from 1 to n-1, would divide up, with half being residues and the other half, non-residues. Even better, a type of inversion is found: Halfway through the n-1 residues of a modulus of n, the residues would turn around and repeat themselves backwards—or as Bach would say, a *canon al roversio*.

Next, the modulae would divide into two different basic groups of prime numbers. Modulae such as 5, 13 and 17 would fall into one group, called the "4n+1" primes, where each residue had a unique partner, whereby their sum would equal the modulus. (In mod 13, 1 pairs with 12, 4 with 9, 3 with 10.) However, the residue of modulae such as 7, 11 and 19, called the "4n+3" primes, would never have such a residue partner; however, each residue did have such a unique partner amongst the non-residues. (For mod 7 in above example, 6, 3 and 5 are the non-residues that pair, in order, with 1, 4 and 2.) Also, the "4n+1" group always includes n-1 as one of its residues, while the "4n+3" group never does. (For example, mod 13 includes 12 as a residue, while mods 7 and 11 do not include 6 and 10, respectively.) Who knew that prime numbers fell into two such categories? But hold on to your horses.

Gauss proved a fundamental principle of reciprocity amongst the two basic groups of prime modulae, raising inversion to a bold new level. How does a modulus relate to its residue if their roles are reversed? (For example, since 13 is a quadratic residue of mod 23, will 23 be a quadratic residue in mod 13? In this case, 23 in mod 13 is the same as 10, and 10 is a quadratic residue of mod 13.) Inversions can be challenging. A too simple example would be to compare two processes: a) given that one knows who the murderer is, figuring out the steps taken by the murderer, vs. b) not knowing any murderer, coming across a murder scene and coming up with the unique sequence of actions that resulted in all the parts (including the identity of the murderer) being as they are. Deducing a chain of events is not quite the job that its inverse is.

(Continued on next page)

III. Chladni's Harmonic Patterns and Ben Franklin

The following year, 1808, Paris was seized with the provocative and beautiful displays by Ernst Chladni of the harmonic patterns of plates bowed with a violin bow. Chladni would spread sand upon a surface, so that when the plate was agitated by the stroke of the violin bow on its edge, the sand would congregate upon the nodal lines—thus, displaying the architecture of the dynamics of the plate.[6] The plates—whether of wood, glass or metal—were only a first approximation of the more complex dynamics of an arched (or "vaulted") violin plate.

Chladni described that he had gotten the idea from Georg Lichtenberg, the Leibnizian professor at the University of Göttingen, who had employed various powders, including sulphur filings, to display the patterns of electrical activity on a surface, activity initiated by the discharge of a spark. Lichtenberg, in turn, had been inspired by America's Benjamin Franklin to investigate electrical and magnetic phenomena.[7] Chladni also credits Göttingen's professor of music, J. N. Forkel, for giving him the idea of using a violin bow for his experiments.[8] Forkel also provoked Chladni to attempt a further development of Franklin's

6. Take a moment to examine the formation of the Chladni patterns: https://youtu.be/lRFysSAxWxI

7. Lichtenberg was a student at Göttingen when Benjamin Franklin visited in 1766. Lichtenberg attended the welcome dinner for Franklin, where he heard Abraham Kaestner's keynote address on Franklin's electrical experiments. Later, Lichtenberg would install Franklin's lightning rods at Göttingen.

8. Johann Nikolaus Forkel was an associate of two of Bach's sons. His early, brief biography of Bach has not been surpassed.

Quadratic Reciprocity and Political Revolutions

(Continued from previous page)

Gauss was able to prove the amazing result about this inversion, one called quadratic reciprocity:

1. Amongst the 4n+1 prime modulae, the modulus is a quadratic residue of every one of its own residues, and it is a quadratic non-residue of all of its non-residues. Very symmetric.
2. Amongst the 4n+3 prime modulae, the modulus is a quadratic residue of its 4n+1 quadratic residues, but a non-residue of its 4n+3 residues. Rather anti-symmetric.
3. Further, amongst the 4n+3 prime modulae, the modulus will be a quadratic residue of its non-quadratic, 4n+3 residues; but will not be a quadratic residue of one of its non-quadratic, 4n+1 residues.[1]

Mastering the symmetries and dissymmetries of the harmonic patterns of Gauss's *Disquisitiones Arithmeticae* were at the root of the work of Germain, Dirichlet, Abel, Galois and Riemann—work on the solar system, Chladni plates, Fermat's Last Theorem, the quintic (or the problem of the boundary at the "fifth-power"), shock-waves, general relativity and, yes, good political revolutions.

So, perhaps the last word here on Gauss's quadratic reciprocity may be allowed for a good political revolutionary:

All consistent mathematics as such, reflects obviously underlying ontological, axiomatic-like presumptions, which, however strenuously "pure" mathematicians may attempt to hide this fact, are "secretions" rooted in the physical geometry inherent in the processes of the individual human thinking mind… [I]t is obvious to me that the real foundation for Gauss's argument for the startling expression of quadratic reciprocity, reflects the implicit reality, that the assumptions of arithmetic are not pure, but, as many of us have insisted, repeatedly over generations, lie within the domain of the ultimately physical geometry of the biology and metabiology of the human mind-function.[2]

—David Shavin

1. This is as far as this brief summary will go. For a much fuller development, see Peter Martinson's 2008 "Quadratic Reciprocity." Otherwise, a useful chart (the one in color) may be found at: https://en.wikipedia.org/wiki/Quadratic_reciprocity.

2. Lyndon LaRouche, "The State of our Union: The End of our Delusion!" *EIR*, Aug. 31, 2007. Page 81. Available at Amazon: https://www.amazon.com/State-Our-Union-End-Delusion-ebook/dp/B01N2ZRDVL/ref=sr_1_1?s=digital-text&ie=UTF8&qid=1518549427&sr=1-1&keywords=The+State+of+Our+Union.+The+End+of+Our+Delusion.

Vibrations created on a Chladni plate with a violin bow produce nodal lines in sand.

musical invention, the glass armonica.[9] Hence, one can view Chladni as an intellectual grandson of Franklin both scientifically, through Lichtenberg, and musically, through Forkel.[10]

Chladni drew the sand patterns that arose from drawing a bow across the edge of the plate.

Chladni published his *Discoveries in the Theory of Sound* in 1787, and displayed his experiments in various cities in Europe.[11] In 1793, he spent a couple of months with Lichtenberg discussing electricity and acoustics. Further, his visit resulted in opening up Paris to Chladni. Fortu-

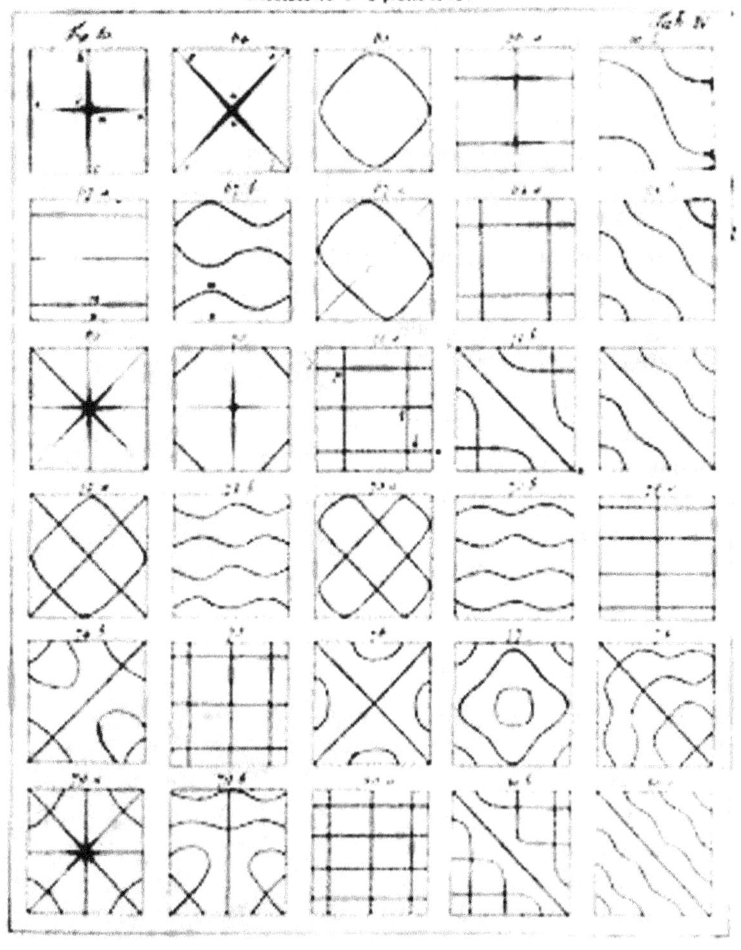

From an 1802 edition of Chladni's Akustik.

nately, there had been a recent fireball in the sky over Göttingen in 1791, but the received view of the event—and, in general at that time, of meteors—was that they had to be the effluvia from volcanos. It seemed outlandish that rocks would be flying down from outside the Earth. Lichtenberg had Chladni spend time in the Göttingen library analyzing reports of various sightings, and computing trajectories, so as to prove the unearthly origin of meteors. Chladni's results, in his 1794 "Eisenmessen" report ("On the origin of the Mass of Iron... and other Ironmasses"), was not immediately accepted. But, in 1803, when the French Minister of the Interior commissioned the physicist, astronomer, and mathematician Jean-Baptiste Biot to investigate the recent meteor shower over L'Aigle, Biot confirmed Chladni's analysis—opening up an audience for Chladni in France.

---

9. Chladni created his instrument, the "euphony," by replacing Franklin's rotating hollow glasses with tuned, cylindrical glass rods tuned at different pitches. Instead of rubbing the glasses with one's fingers, the rods could be initiated by pressing keys and, also, were more reliable in the resultant tone.

10. Of note, Chladni's work was most intensively studied and developed by the Weber brothers, Wilhelm and Ernst. Riemann, who was fascinated with his time spent in Wilhelm Weber's laboratory, furthered both Chladni's and Weber's work in acoustics with his famous "Shock Wave" paper of 1859 ("On the Propagation of Plane Air Waves of Finite Amplitude"). Riemann's student, Eugenio Beltrami, continued this tradition with his work on laminar flow.

11. When in Weimar, Chladni impressed Goethe, who proceeded to study his *Die Akustik*. Goethe reported to Schiller: "Doctor Chladni has arrived and brought his complete *Acoustics* in a quarto volume. I have already read half of it and shall give you a somewhat agreeable oral report on its content, substance, method, and form."

IV. Chladni's Harmonics: Excites Germain, Depresses LaGrange

In 1808, Gaspard Monge introduced Chladni's research to the Institute of France, where Chladni performed his experiment for its Class of Physical Sciences and Mathematics. All factions were provoked by what they saw, and Pierre-Simon Laplace arranged for Chladni, in February 1809, to repeat the presentation for Napoleon. Among those present were Biot, Felix Savart and Alexander von Humboldt. Chladni wrote that there was an awareness, including by Napoleon, that "one is not yet able to apply a calculation to areas curved in more than one direction"—or what can be described as the "arched-violin" problem—and Napoleon called for the matter to be made the subject of a prize contest.

The reigning French authority in mathematics, Joseph-Louis Lagrange, declared that the known mathematics was not capable of accounting for the harmonic patterns displayed by Chladni. Sophie Germain reported that, prior to Chladni's visit, she had studied Chladni's works, but had been discouraged by Lagrange: "As soon as I learned about M. Chladni's first experiments, it seemed to me that analysis could determine the laws that govern. But I chanced to learn from a great geometer [Lagrange] whose first works had been devoted to the theory of sound, that this problem contained difficulties that I had not even suspected. I stopped thinking about it. Seeing M. Chladni's experiments during his stay in Paris excited my interest anew."

Ernst Chladni

V. Harmony—The Attractive and Repulsive Actions of Molecules?

The Laplace/Lagrange faction formulated the prize contest called for by Napoleon according to their own ideological constrictions: Mathematical equations were to be developed that would account for the harmonic patterns of Chladni, but the equations should stem from the linear foundation established by Leonhard Euler's investigation of a vibrating bar. That is, entrants to the contest were to master Euler's treatment of a one-dimensional vibration, and then build upon that to account for the two-dimensional plate. They simply ignored the fact that Chladni had already shown, experimentally, that Euler's formula for the vibration rate, even for the one-dimensional case of a rod vibrating back and forth, was incorrect. (Chladni also showed that Giordano Riccati's correction of Euler was correct.[12]) Laplace's faction thought they had a champion for their cause, who could cook the numbers in their favor—Laplace's protégé, Siméon Denis Poisson.

In 1807, two years prior, Laplace had assigned Poisson the job of providing a mathematical cover for Laplace's defense of Isaac Newton. Empirical measurements of the speed of sound waves through air had refused to obey Newton's theory. Laplace, as recounted by Biot, had manufactured an "ingenious explanation of this difficulty by attributing the acceleration of sound to changes in temperature experienced by the particles of air as they condense and dilate." Poisson was supposed to buttress Laplace's defense of Newton by working out the mathematics of this model. The effort failed, but the intent of this faction was clear. The 1809 contest on Chladni's harmonics was to pose yet another opportunity to defend the Newtonian program of building up from fundamental particles and imputed forces, and then cooking the numbers to justify the defense.

However, none of their faction could actually generate a mathematical accounting that cohered with the harmonic patterns. Fortunately, Germain was never trained deeply enough in the technical manipulations of their faction, and it worked to her benefit. Though her entry was hampered by having to couch matters in the "Euler"-ian terms of the contest, she had the charming

---

12. Riccati's correction of Euler is found in his *Treatise on Elastic Fibres*. Of some interest, Riccati had also composed an "Essay on the Counterpoint Laws," and his musical collaborator, Andrea Luchesi, was the Kapellmeister in Bonn during Beethoven's youth.

insight to construct her analysis around the interaction of the two principal (maximum and minimum) curvatures of the Chladni plates in action.

Laplace, in a note to his 1809 "Memoire" on the subject, articulated the Newtonian ideology standing in the way, in his dismissal of an approach based upon the physical curvature: "In order to determine the equilibrium and movement of an elastic, naturally straight lamina that is bent into an arbitrary curve, it has been assumed that at each point its stiffness is inversely proportional to its radius of curvature. But this law is only secondary and derives from the attractive and repulsive actions of molecules, which are a function of distance."[13] For their faction, everything stemmed from fundamentally unknown hard balls interacting by means of a fundamentally unknown attraction or repulsion.

A letter drafted by Germain records her thoughts at the time: "But by far the greatest obstacle to the progress of science and to the undertaking of new tasks and provinces therein is found in this: that men despair and think things impossible... [I do not see] any strong objections to my theory other than the improbability of having it meet with justice. I fear, however, the influence of opinion that M. Lagrange expressed. Without doubt, the problem has been abandoned only because this grand geometer judged it difficult. Possibly this same prejudgment will mean a condemnation of my work without a reflective examination...."

The lawful result was that Poisson, and anyone else following the lead of Laplace, could not even formulate a presentable entry. By the 1811 deadline, Sophie Germain was the only entrant. She was denied the prize, as she had an insufficient grasp of the differential calculus. The contest was renewed, and two years later, with still no other entrants, she was given an honorable mention. Then, finally, she was awarded the "prix extraordinaire" for the 1815 contest, for her "Memoir on the Vibrations of Elastic Plates." Even then, the committee grudgingly admitted that her general equation had accounted for the Chladni harmonic patterns rather well, but added the disclaimer that they could not endorse her analytical method. They stated: "The differential equation given by the author is correct [in predicting the harmonics] although it has not resulted from the experimental demonstration." That is, she had not "built up" the mathe-

matics from the hard facts, but rather had worked out her general equation from her physical hypothesis. Germain understood what was going on and posed the pointed followup question to the committee: Since her general equation came from her hypothesis regarding the principal curvatures, was that also incorrect? Her motto she had chosen to head her 1815 submission was from Virgil: "Fortunate is one who is able to know the causes of things."

The contest regarding Chladni's strange and beautiful harmonic patterns was now put aside. The Academy did not publish her prize-winning paper. The approach Germain had taken in her paper was largely ignored; and for Germain's last sixteen years, she was more tolerated than taken seriously. This year, 1815, was the beginning of the Restoration in France, when the Bourbon dynasty was re-established. The Ecole Polytechnique lost the leadership of Gaspard Monge and Lazare Carnot, and the reign of Augustin-Louis Cauchy over French science began. Over the next fifteen years, that reign would keep Germain too isolated, and would actively suppress the work of the other "poet-mathematician" students of Gauss's *Disquisitiones Arithmeticae*, the young geniuses, Niels Abel and Evariste Galois.

VI. Gaussian Curvature and Industrial Banking

We shall cite one provocative case as to what might have been, had Germain been able to benefit from any normal scientific exchanges. Just as Germain, in 1815, submitted her prize-winning paper on Chladni, a student of Monge at the Ecole, one Benjamin Olinde Rodrigues, attained his doctorate. He had developed tools in the rigorous treatment of intrinsic curvature that would have greatly benefitted Germain. His intrinsic curvature and his "total curvature" were more famously and thoroughly developed a decade later by Gauss (in his 1827 "Theorema Egregium" and his "Disquisitiones generales circa superficies curvas"), and is now referred to as "Gaussian curvature." Even allowing for her use of the prevailing extrinsic measurements of curvature, Germain's weakness in her treatment of the unified measurement of the maximum and minimum curvatures of the doubly-curved surface was her adoption of the arithmetic mean (and not the product) of the two curvatures. However, Germain would not hear of Gauss's developments on curvature until 1829; and in the reaction of 1815, Rodrigues, a Jew from Bordeaux, had no career in

---

13. Of note, in 1814, Lazare Carnot weighed in, promoting a memoir by one Paul Réné Binet, who had cited Lagrange's rectilinear formulation as failing to take account, even in the case of the one-dimensional vibrating bar of Euler, of the more complex torque component.

mathematics open to him—and it appears that Germain was not able to benefit from his work either.

Even so, it were still possible that Germain and Rodrigues could have collaborated outside of the Ecole Polytechnique or the Academy of Sciences. Blocked from a teaching position, Rodrigues and his brother set up a "national banking" salon that might have overlapped with Germain's father, himself a former directeur of the Banque de France. The salon included: Jacques Laffitte, also a former directeur of the Banque de France, and a proponent of industry and railroads; Vital Roux, a regent of the Banque de France, whose pamphlets agitated for directing credit toward industry; and Emile and Isaac Pereire, cousins of Rodrigues. (The technical consultant at the Pereires' industrial concern, Michel Chevalier, was Galois' friend. His brother, Auguste, was the one who saved Galois' works.) Rodrigues himself would be key in the development of France's first operating railroad, similar to the role in Prussia of August Crelle, the sponsor of Niels Abel. It were quite possible that Germain's father socialized with these industrial- and science-connected bankers, however no link with Rodrigues' national-banking salon has yet been established—and no evidence of Rodrigues' introduction of the intrinsic measurement of curvature detected in Germain's work.

VII. Germain and the New, Young Poet-Mathematicians

With the exception of Bernhard Riemann, Germain had more direct interchange with Gauss than the other three leading students of Gauss's *DA*. And she was more centrally placed than any of the other four, to potentially serve as a focal point for their work. Dirichlet, Abel and Galois came to, or were in, Paris between 1822 and 1832, where Germain was the leading student of Gauss over the last two decades. However, as a woman, she did not have proper standing amongst the scientific community to make such a collaboration naturally develop. Dirichlet, Abel and Galois would find Paris a forbidding and hostile environment. Only Dirichlet survived the experience.

Dirichlet was in Paris from 1822 to 1827, and both he and Germain used Gauss's *DA* to work on Fermat's Last Theorem, and on the problem of the quintic—that is, why algorithms, or generalized mechanical solutions, of algebraic equations broke down at the fifth power, as if running up against an unseen barrier. Be-

ginning in May 1823, Germain was finally allowed to attend and listen to presentations of the Academy, being provided with tickets by the Academy Secretary, Jean-Baptiste Fourier. She probably attended Dirichlet's presentation on Fermat, made to the Academy in July 1825. She herself had prepared a twenty-page memoir on Fermat's Last Theorem several years earlier, telling Gauss in 1819 that his *DA* was the basis of her strategy. And two months after Dirichlet's 1825 presentation, Germain's correspondent, Legendre, presented his followup to Dirichlet to the Academy, one that included a mention of Germain's work. It seems probable that Germain and Dirichlet would have met and discussed their work, but no record of such is known.

What is known is that in May 1825, Germain finally meets, in person, with Guglielmo Libri, an Italian student of the *DA* who had been in touch with Germain since 1819, but now had travelled to Paris. Libri presents his work before the Academy on June 13, 1825, several weeks prior to Dirichlet. Libri would be Germain's closest collaborator between 1825 and 1831. He was to become both the author of her biography and the preserver of her work. Libri had a very colorful life, one that is beyond the scope of this series.

Germain ended up, in the 1820s, having to publish on her own her works on the Chladni plates. Her papers submitted to the Academy were not published, nor even provided a courtesy review.[14] It wasn't until 1828 that an article of hers was finally published by a scientific journal—*Annales de chimie et de physique*, edited by François Arago and Joseph Louis Gay-Lussac, had the honor.[15] There, on the subject of the dynamics of elasticity (of laminar surfaces, such as the Chladni plates), Germain reminded her readers of her overlooked approach, and explained why Siméon Poisson's much-promoted approach was inadequate, and referred the readers to her self-published 1826 report on elastic surfaces, one that Cauchy had suppressed at the Academy.

The infamy of Cauchy in actively working to crush Niels Abel and Evariste Galois, the youthful geniuses of Gauss's *Disquisitiones Arithmeticae*, was covered earlier in this series.[16] However, it was in the weeks immediately prior to Cauchy's burial of Abel's work, that

---

14. Germain's 1824 "*Effets dus a l'epaisseur plus ou moins grande des plaques elastiques*" was assigned for review, but was buried. Her 1825 paper assimilating recent developments in acoustics (including those of Charles Wheatstone) was simply ignored.

15. See Germain's 1828 article at https://babel.hathitrust.org/cgi/pt?id=hvd.hx3dvx;view=1up;seq=131

16. See footnote 1.

Cauchy was already at work on Germain's case. On July 7, 1826, Germain sent a long letter to Cauchy, reviewing how developments since 1815 only strengthen her physical-hypothesis approach, and undercut the Newtonian approach. There, she refuted Poisson's molecular explanation, explaining further that, regarding elastic bodies, imbedded assumptions about the molecules are useless and even harmful.

Fiinally, she took apart Felix Savart's experiments, even though Cauchy would still use them as support for his own work. Cauchy relied upon Savart, who had won his entry into the Academy circles a few years earlier with his bizarre, flat violin, one designed in the shape of a trapezoid! Here, a picture is worth a thousand words—the trapezoidal violin was emblematic of the problems with this faction. Savart's obsession for maximizing the vibrations of small parts ended up in a big failure.[17] Germain wrote of the celebrated Savart: "This Monsieur Savart would have been able to help me a lot if he wanted to use the kind of sagacity with which he is endowed with good experiments on curved surfaces."[18] Cauchy did acknowledge receipt of both Germain's letter and the memoir that she had submitted to the Academy, but no more. Fourier, the Academy's Secretary, told Germain that Cauchy was assigned to report on her memoir, but Cauchy never gave that report. Within weeks, with the submission to Cauchy of Abel's magnum opus, Cauchy would graduate to become the infamous serial abuser of Gauss's students.

VIII. Germain's Swan Song—Her Last Two 'Gauss' Papers

Niels Abel died in 1829 at the age of twenty-six. In 1830, his mentor, colleague and publisher, August Crelle, visited Germain. Crelle came from Berlin, on a mission in collaboration with the Humboldt brothers, to

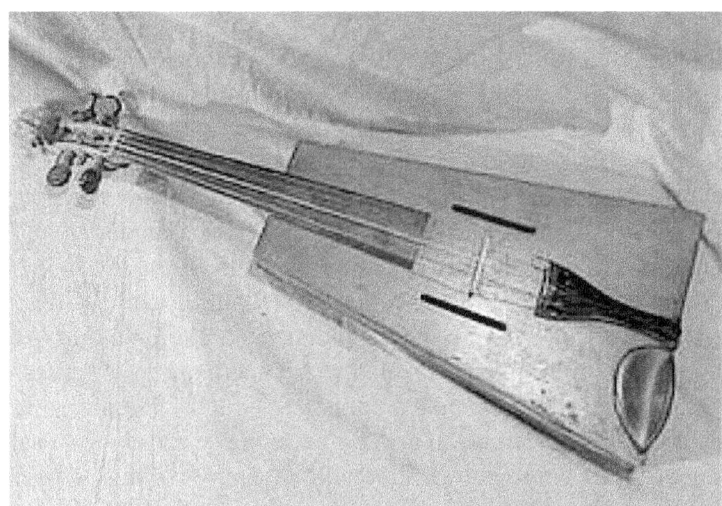

By eliminating the upper and lower chambers of the violin for a simpler trapezoidal box, Savart aimed to maximize the amount of vibrations at the surface. He only had to sacrifice the beauty of a lased, bel canto *sound.*

study what methods the Ecole Polytechnique had used to build up a national science program. Crelle was impressed with Germain and agreed to publish her works in Berlin. Sophie raced against time, and debilitating pain, as she was dying from a cancer detected the previous year. The two works that she chose to leave the world were both based upon Gauss: a memoir on the curvature of surfaces and a summary of the original material that she had sent Gauss in 1804.[19]

The previous year, in early 1829, Gauss had instructed his student Bader to deliver a copy of his *Theoria residuorum biquadraticorum* [Theory of Quadratic Residues] to Germain. She reported back to Gauss, March 28, 1829: "I have read, with great pleasure, your memoir on biquadratic residues, which this young scientist has given me on your behalf." Germain then briefed Bader on her own work, which prompted a discussion of Gauss's latest work on curvature. Bader brought out "the learned memoir in which you compare the curvature of surfaces to that of the sphere (Gauss's 1827 "Disquisitiones generales circa superficies curvas")... [General Investigations of Curved Surfaces.] I cannot tell you, Monsieur, how astonished, and at the same time, how satisfied I was in learning that a renowned mathematician, almost simultaneously, had

---

17. A real violin is designed with an upper and lower chamber, on the model of the head and chest cavities used in "bel canto" singing. The dynamics involved in the coupling of the resonances of the two chambers is not built up from percussive interactions of hard bodies. See the author's unpublished 2010 report, "Leibniz's Dynamics & Stradivari's 'Bel Canto' Violin Breakthrough."

18. For her own experiments, Germain had employed a skilled mechanic named Mons Moulfarine, to make thin glass plates of varying curvatures and thicknesses.

19. In her work on curvature, she had employed a formula for the radius of curvature of an oblique surface that had been developed by the student of Monge, Charles Dupin—covered earlier in this series as a model for Edgar Alan Poe in his treatment of Galois. (It is unclear what Germain knew of Dupin, as she attributed his formula, mistakenly, to Jean Baptiste Meusnier.)

the idea of an analogy that seems to me so rational that I neither understood how no one had thought of it sooner, nor how no one has wished to give any attention to date to what I have already published in this regard."

But Bader and Germain don't have enough time to get everything resolved. Bader does not have a duplicate copy of the curvature paper to leave with Germain, so she has not been able to fully digest Gauss's work. (Apparently, in determining the radius for her referent sphere, she was still employing the arithmetic mean of the minimal and maximal curvatures.) She tells Gauss of Poisson's objections to her approach: He was "relying on Euler's discussion of the infinite number of different curves obtained from the intersections of different planes passing through a given point of the surface" and he "had thought that I had not sufficiently established the choice of principal curvatures.... I am in the process of proving, in a superior way relative to what I have published previously in this regard, that whatever be the shape of the element of the surface, that is to say, whatever be the manner in which the curvature of the element is distributed about the point of tangency, the force that would be employed to destroy the curvature of this element remains constant.... I regret ... not being able to submit to your judgment a multitude of ideas that I have not published and that would take too long to write out."

In her last few months, Germain did have the satisfaction of finally seeing her two works published in a major scientific journal. Her work on curvature was composed in 1830, ironically, during the few days of the turmoil of the July Revolution. Perhaps a coincidence, but once again—as when during the violence of July 1789, the thirteen-year-old girl found sanctuary in her father's library and found the genius of the endangered Archimedes—Sophie accessed her inner voice.[20]

The French government highlights the life and work of Sophie Germain in this 2016 postage stamp.

IX. The Science of 'Different Modalities'—Transcendental Music, Bach and Gauss

Sophie Germain died on Monday, June 27, 1831.[21] In her last letter to Libri, a month before her death, she expressed her conviction of the unity of art and science: "Ah! No doubt, the sciences, literature and fine arts were born of one and the same sentiment. They reproduced, according to the means that are the essence of each of them, copies of their constantly renewed innate style, a universal type of truth, that is so strongly imprinted in superior minds." What informed, drove and sustained Germain, during her long battle for the beauties of Chladni's harmonic pictures, was her music— and her unwillingness to betray the beauty of the inner soul.

The role of music in Germain's life is simply not mentioned in the accounts of her approach to the Chladni plates, though it is painfully obvious, during the long battle for her approach, that she would not allow the harmonic patterns to be reduced to things that go bump in the night. In 1833, Germain's nephew, De Lachevardière, published her thoughts on these matters in a work entitled *Considerations generales sur l'état des sciences et des lettres aux differentes époques de leur culture*. Libri explains about this posthumous work, that "...among her papers have been found some very subtle philosophical reflections, for she was actively occupied with metaphysics, which she claimed was the source of the true philosophical spirit. She thought very little of diverse philosophical systems.... [She had] an ability

---

old ideas, she wrote her '*Memoire sur la Courbure des Surfaces*,' which appeared in the *Annales* of M. Crelle of Berlin."

21. In Paris, seventeen days later, Galois was arrested and jailed, leading to his death at the age of twenty. Though barely fifty-five, Germain actually lived longer than her four, compatriot, Gaussian "poet-mathematicians." In her last two years, Sophie lamented the death of Abel and the unappreciated genius of Galois.

---

20. Her biographer Libri puts it: "When the revolution of July broke out, she took refuge in her study as she had during that of '89; it was during the week of fighting that, taking up and developing further some

… to reconcile similarities between the physical order and the moral order, which she regarded as subject to the same laws."

Amongst her extended reflections on the gap between the scientific pursuit of truth and the emotional level of her culture, Germain argues for an underlying unity of beauty and truth. In her words:

"The oracles of taste and the dictates of reason are similar; order, proportion, and simplicity never cease to be intellectual necessities. Their subjects are different, but the judgment is constantly based on the same universal type, which belongs equally to the beautiful and to the truth."[22]

"A trait of genius … in the sciences, in the fine arts, or in literature, all have the same effect of making us happy for the same reason: they reveal to us all sorts of relationships that have escaped us. We are suddenly transported into a high region where we discover a new ordering of ideas and of emotions."

In the work, Germain expresses a deep-seated fear of the outbreak of violent emotions as displayed in the 1789-94 turmoil (and, possibly, also from the events of July 1830). She argues that leaders have not been sufficiently developed to deal with revolutions. Decent leaders in normal times are clever enough. "In times of crisis, however, it's something else. Circumstances become pressing; we must know how to make prompt decisions; we also often need courage, and courage is not necessarily a quality of the clever man. Society runs a thousand dangers which are as difficult to avoid as they are to predict." How might we unite genius and courage? It turns out that it is a too rarely-exercised transcendental power that is required, one that Germain knows well from the mastery of modalities displayed by Gauss's *DA*.

Then, somewhat surprisingly, Sophie singles out the missing ingredient in France and in Europe—the musical equivalent of what she has heard in Gauss's "poetry." She argues that, while music has the universal power of being able to "strike at the truth for the least educated man," it also takes work to master the harmonic whole. This necessary work has been avoided "because of the prejudice that separates music from the field of intelligence." The educated might achieve a certain level of

literacy, but it lacks rigor. But "with respect to music, things are quite different." While some of the educated may even come to appreciate many effects in music, this is still below the mastering, e.g., the overlooked genius of Bach's well-tempered system. "Today, we no longer understand what history has given us through the teaching of the different modalities. Therefore, how could we ever be conscious of this when music is only considered as the art of caressing the ear? How could music be the object of serious attention when it is reduced to such an exclusive use? … Music is completely metaphysical."

X. In Conclusion: Genius and Happiness—Or, Playing Ping-Pong with the Stars

Sophie Germain knew quite well what it was like to have her scientific work treated as the curiosities of a woman caressing the ear of the scientific establishment. That did not deter her from her mission.

She heard in Gauss's "poetry" a revival of Bach's unified development of the different modalities, and thought her culture was suffering from the retreat from Bach's level of science. Gauss's treatment of the hidden truths uniting the modalities was a pathway for civilization to train its leaders to deal with revolutionary stresses and revolutionary solutions.

Gauss's uniquely rigorous examination of what seem to be the completely familiar 1, 2, and 3's of arithmetic, uncovers profound insights as to how the human mind works when it ventures to order the world. Sophie Germain thinks this is key to the pursuit of happiness: "A trait of genius … in the sciences, in the fine arts, or in literature, all have the same effect of making us happy for the same reason: they reveal to us all sorts of relationships that have escaped us. We are suddenly transported into a high region where we discover a new ordering of ideas and of emotions."

Lyndon and Helga LaRouche think that Americans can still engage in this pursuit of happiness, should they forgive themselves for a few decades of becoming small and petty, and allow themselves to seize the historic opportunity of the great infrastructure projects of the Belt and Road. We would discover "all sorts of relationships that have escaped us" and find ourselves "suddenly transported into a high region where we discover a new ordering of ideas and of emotions."

---

22. Pierre Beaudry has kindly provided the translations of key portions of Germain's *Considerations generales*.… I told him of my suspicions that evidence of Germain's reliance upon beauty and music for her scientific work might lie within the work, and he immediately tracked down the relevant content.

May 18, 2005

ON THE NOËTIC PRINCIPLE

Vernadsky and Dirichlet's Principle

by Lyndon H. LaRouche, Jr.

The following is prompted by an examination of an implicitly accredited English translation of V.I. Vernadsky's 1935 On Some Fundamental Problems of Biogeochemistry, *secured through the Columbia University files contributed by V.I. Vernadsky's son, Professor George Vernadsky, New Haven, Conn., U.S.A.*

It is an often demonstrated fact of recent generations of European history, that certain victims of their classroom studies of Classical Greek, would have never understood any crucial concept of Plato's work, including the significance of the English term *Noëtic* as adopted from Academician V.I. Vernadsky's definition of the *Noösphere.*[1] The common source of the errors of all varieties of such failed former students of classroom Greek, and of many more others, still today, has been their disposition to look up definitions in dictionaries or by quoting so-called authorities, *rather than actually experiencing the relevant conception by replicating the original author's presentation of the process of generating the relevant discovery, as Vernadsky himself illustrated this method for acquiring knowledge of fundamental physical principles in the 1935 writing to which I refer here.*

Such has been my experience of most of the putatively learned and other failed modern commentators on the argument presented by Vernadsky, or also by others on related subject matters.

Indeed, most of the crucial conceptions of valid science in globally extended European civilization today, are to be traced from their implied origin in the pre-Aristotelean Classical Greek, as from Thales and the

Pythagoreans through the works of Plato. The conceptions of *Biosphere* and *Noösphere* developed by Academician Vernadsky, are a case in point. These conceptions, which Vernadsky associated with the Classical Greek tradition, could not be adequately understood except in those historical terms of reference to Plato's actually intended, non-reductionist usage of the Classical Greek for stating principles of discovery illustrated in the 1935 paper considered here.

What Plato actually refers to by such relevant terms, is to be known, not by reading a glossary, but by experiencing the actual act of discovery which solves the puzzle which Plato's argument presents in locations such as his pro-Heracleitus, **Parmenides** dialogue; only if the reader of that dialogue were a pedant, or a pompous fool such as G.W.F. Hegel, ignorant of the ABCs of the creative experience, would he have ever contested the authenticity of Plato's authorship of that dialogue.

The same point is illustrated by the appalling thick-headedness of Lagrange's attempted public refutation of that attack on his folly which had been delivered in Carl F. Gauss's 1799 dissertation. The point is also illustrated by the standard act of classroom stupidity imitated by those literally millions of victims, who, in the course of times past, have swallowed arch-reductionist Augustin Cauchy's epistemologically childish "limit theorem."

Over the decades since the fact of the existence of V.I. Vernadsky's work first became known to me, near the close of the 1940s, I, looking as if out of the corner of my eye, had come slowly to recognize that his most celebrated contributions had a certain potential relevance to my own independent discoveries in the field of a science of physical economy. That gradual recogni-

---

1. For example, the contrary meanings associated with Plato and Aristotle, respectively.

Writes LaRouche: "The characteristics of the Biosphere, as Vernadsky … defined it, and Noösphere, as I define physical economies as wholes, are analogous. Everything to which I have referred, on this account, in excerpting Vernadsky's 1935 paper, has a parallel in my methods of a science of physical economy." Left: R&D at Lockheed Martin Corp. for the International Thermonuclear Experimental Reactor—the energy source of the future. Above: Vladimir I. Vernadsky (1863-1945).

tion began more than fifty years ago, in the course of the continuing initial development of my own principled contributions. So, over decades, as more of his work came, as if piece by piece, gradually to my attention, I had come to recognize that he had already offered an overview which was compatible, in principle, with certain discoveries which I had experienced during the initial phases of development of my own Leibnizian notion of physical economy as such.[2]

As Vernadsky defines the guidelines for a biogeochemical investigation of the boundaries separating the biosphere categorically from the abiotic domain, I had, as I explain below, developed my own, somewhat parallel approach to this view, that in work in which I, working from my standpoint as an admirer of Leibniz, subsumed the principled distinctions separating the principle of human scientific creativity from both animal and abiotic modes of behavior. However, until some work which my association did during the mid-1970s, I made no significant effort to incorporate the Vernadsky legacy directly into our work on the princi-

---

2. For those not yet familiar with these facts, an actually scientific conception of economic processes was originally discovered, and developed, as a science of physical economy, as a branch of physical science, a science needed to replace and supersede the then pre-existing modern doctrines of what was known as cameralism. On the record, this development was done exclusively by Gottfried Leibniz during the interval 1671-1716. It was the influence of Leibniz's discoveries which informed the crucial features of the development of that American System of political-economy which latter has been the chief rival and adversary of the British system, world wide, ever since. My own original discoveries, as a follower of Leibniz in this field, were developed by me, during 1948 and later, in continuing reaction against the radical reductionist follies of Norbert Wiener's argument for "information theory," in his 1948 *Cybernetics*. Over that interval of these original discoveries in the field of

physical economy, 1948-1953, my adversarial targets had included the relevant work, on the founding of what became known as the "ivory tower" school of mathematical economics, of Bertrand Russell follower Wiener's co-thinker John von Neumann, as illustrated by von Neumann's and Oskar Morgenstern's *Theory of Games and Economic Behavior*. Von Neumann's posthumously published Yale lectures on the subject of *The Computer and the Brain*, are of crucial implicit significance in reading von Neumann's lunatic, long-winded argument respecting economy. On the record, my methods have been, contrary to the British school and its positivist fanatics, the most successful approach to long-range economic forecasting of the recent forty-odd years.

Lyndon LaRouche (left) lectures on April 28, 1994 at Pobisk Kuznetsov's "President" program, held at the Russian Academy of Sciences in Moscow. On the right, Dr. Kuznetsov in the audience. Writes LaRouche of Kuznetsov, who died in 2001: "I, like many who knew him and his work, miss him very much today."

ples of physical economy. Even those efforts of the 1970s touched Vernadsky's work in a passing, peripheral, if useful way.

It was only from 1994 on, through benefits of my associations with two now-departed Russian friends, the most remarkable Professor Taras Muranivsky and the scientist Pobisk Kuznetzov, among others, that I grew more confident of the existence of special, crucially important affinities between Academician Vernadsky's and my own lines of work in redefining a science of physical economy. The agreement, and some points of disagreement, in my own and Pobisk's views, were presented to a relevant Moscow scientific audience during that period.[3] In materials bearing on Vernadsky's

work which were subsequently made available to me through some of my associates, I was convinced that I had sufficient evidence to draw out those connections between my own work and Vernadsky's which were featured in my 2001 ***The Economics of the Noösphere***.[4] The evidence then in hand was sufficient to have shown me that the problem implicitly resolved by his argument, as known to me then, was largely congruent with my own original discoveries in the field of a science of physical economy.

However, even then, during the late 1990s and beyond, while I was certain of the validity of Vernadsky's statement describing the central features of his stated notion of the Noösphere, I had yet to discover evidence satisfying me in respect to some important details of his approach to his original discovery of that conception.[5]

---

3. The debated issue on that occasion was on the definition of "energy." My host, Pobisk, began his lecture by defending the standard reductionist doctrine on that subject, and challenged me to define my principle of anti-entropy accordingly. In my turn, I opposed that definition of "energy" on that occasion, as many other occasions, before and after. The misguided suspicion in certain Soviet scientific insider circles studying my own original proposal for a strategic defense initiative had been that I had somehow acquired knowledge of super-secret Soviet work of the 1970s and 1980s, in which Pobisk had been involved, bearing on the scientific feasibility of such an initiative. I had no such knowledge of Soviet secret work, beyond my conviction that certain known lines in Soviet scientific work pointed to their ability to recognize the feasibility of developments along the lines I was proposing. Otherwise, Pobisk and I got along nicely. I, like many who knew him and his work, miss him very much today.

---

4. *The Economics of the Noösphere*. See the work which I referenced in writing that book: ***V.I. Vernadsky: Scientific Thought As A Planetary Phenomenon***, B.A. Starostin, trans. (Moscow: Nongovernmental Ecological V.I. Vernadsky Foundation, 1997). In writing what was published as my 2001 book, I had gone no further than this Starostin translation.

5. One crucial, contributing problem in present-day readings of the work of Vernadsky is to be seen as a carry-over of the earlier influence of the implicitly dionysian "ecology cult" of the Cambridge Systems Analysis group on Soviet ideology during the 1970s and 1980s, an influence wielded through the Laxenberg, Austria International Institute for Applied Systems Analysis (IIASA) by such as the U.S.A.'s McGeorge

itself, the present relevance of this paper for me, is that, in that location, Vernadsky's exhibits emphatically, and repeatedly, the same principle of investigation which underlies what became his later, categorical distinction of the Noösphere from the Biosphere. For both cases, the Biosphere and Noösphere, the common distinction of his method is that otherwise best identified as Bernhard Riemann's emphasis on what he describes as *Dirichlet's Principle*.

I have already emphasized this connection to Riemann in my 2001 ***The Economics of the Noösphere***, that Vernadsky himself identified his view of the Noösphere as systemically Riemannian. Back in 2001, I could confirm this in broad terms, as I did then; but I left room for relevant fine points on this account yet to be discovered. A reading of the recently acquired access to Vernadsky's indicated 1935 paper on biogeochemistry, filled in some important blanks left in the material I had considered for my 2001 report.

EIRNS/Rachel Douglas

1996. It was only from 1994 on, LaRouche writes, through benefit of his association with "the most remarkable Professor Taras Muranivsky and the scientist Pobisk Kuznetzov, among others, that I grew more confident of the existence of special, crucially important affinities between Academician Vernadsky's and my own lines of work in redefining a science of physical economy."

Recently, during the recent fortnight, a collaborator of mine forwarded copies of some translations of Academician Vernadsky's work, work made available through a collection supplied to Columbia University by Vernadsky's son, Professor George Vernadsky. One of these, a 1935 work, "On Some Fundamental Problems of Biogeochemistry," includes a crucial margin of additional validation of my own conclusions respecting the method which underlies Academician Vernadsky's later argument on the distinction of the Noösphere from the Biosphere. I brought a copy of that 1935 paper along with me as a subject of work to be done during my international travels, and have spent happy hours, while shrugging off jet-lag, in doing my literary duty on this account.

Although the subject of this 1935 paper is the distinction of the chemistry of living processes from those of non-living, rather than the subject of the Noösphere

My acquisition and study of the 1935 paper not only leads me to additional observations on the deep quality of Vernadsky's work on the subjects of both the Biosphere and Noösphere. As that work of his bears on the application of the prospects on development of mineral resources, in my recently published work on ***Earth's Next Fifty Years***, everything bearing upon a deeper insight into the implications of Vernadsky's referenced discoveries, is of strategic importance for all humanity today.[6]

Nine Excerpts Considered As One

Immediately below, I have identified nine excerpts from the referenced 1935 Vernadsky paper, which I present now, in sequence, without interrupting that presentation with my own argument, the latter which I have consigned to the elaboration developed following

Bundy, and Britain's Club of Rome figures Dr. Alexander King and Solly Zuckermann. Despite some deferences to the Soviet reductionist school in his references to the history of science in the Starostin translation, Vernadsky's strength lies in his actual work in the fields of his original discoveries in physical science; when he departs from that field, his views on the history of social thought, as on the subject of Plato, as expressed in the Starostin translation, are not always defensible scientifically. This was a cause of my cautious approach, until now, to certain material found in the 1997 text.

6. ***Earth's Next Fifty Years,*** available in paperback or Kindle.

that presentation of the cited excerpts. My intent in this procedure, is to afford readers a general flavor of the point I am emphasizing from within Vernadsky's work, while also pointing the relevant specialists to something which is implicitly of deeper relevance than his work on biogeochemistry as such.

I add, as a preface to presenting those excerpts here, that the nature of the content of the 1935 work, when considered in light of his own later writings known to me on the Noösphere, is such that no significant margin is left for assuming any relevant defects in the English translation which I have consulted in what I have to say here. We are dealing with scientific ideas expressed in ways which rise above the ambiguities of differences in the mother-languages of the medium employed. The validity of the ideas of principle stated is imparted by reliance on the experimental standpoint which the responsible mind must always bring to describing the observed tests of crucial-experimental demonstrations themselves.

However, I caution my readers, in the setting in which I locate Vernadsky's work here, it is my right and obligation to situate my view of his work within the bounds of my own established competence in relevant features of the branch of science known as physical economy. I believe, that by the close of this present report, I will have made clear the relevant lines of division of labor between my own views and his.

First, take the two following, interdependent paragraphs from Section II of his report on the perspectives of the work being conducted at his Laboratory:[7]

"A great part of our work is connected with a study not of the atoms themselves but of chemical elements, of isotopic mixtures. In purely chemical processes all of the isotopes of the same element are manifested in a similar way, Hence, while we remain within the field of purely chemical processes, the chemical element may be identified with the atom, as it is the case in the periodical system of elements. On this the whole chemistry is based.

"Proceeding from this general statement, it has been possible to show by the work of our laboratory that the *atomic composition of organisms, plants and animals is as characteristic a feature as their morphological form or physiological structure* as their appearance and internal structures.... An organism does not show a passive attitude towards the chemical medium; it actively creates atomic composition, it tends to choose, consciously or unconsciously, the chemical elements necessary for life, but as life presents a field of dynamic equilibria, it reflects—both in its composition and in its form—the different physico-chemical properties of the medium. These variations, however, do not change their average, little varying expression."

And, then, in the immediately following paragraph:

"A species established by biologists may be characterized in weight or atomic composition as precisely, as by its morphological features, also within a definite range of variations it may characterize a homogeneous living substance—the totality of organisms of the same species, race, jordanons,—as it is characterized by morphological features. In the average numbers, the amounts of atoms, of chemical elements, composing a living organism, are as constant and as characteristic for it as its form, size, weight, etc. It is possible that in the numerical relations of living beings thus expressed, the same harmonious combinations will be found, which are so distinctly manifest in the vividness of the living nature. They should be probably manifested in harmonious relations of numbers in these natural bodies—in living organisms, as numerical relations are harmoniously manifested in the natural bodies of inert nature—in crystals and minerals. The elucidation of this problem is a task of the nearest future."

Next, take the entirety of the concluding paragraph of the paper's Section II for general background and flavor:

"We have first embraced by the precise methods 18 chemical elements; now, we are able to make a quantitatively precise study of over 60, and we must comprise all of the 92, if not more,[8] for it becomes clearer and clearer that it is in the biosphere that living matter embraces and controls all or nearly all of the chemical elements. All of them *are necessary for life* and not one of them comes to the organism by chance. *There are no special elements peculiar to life.* There are *predominant* elements. When taken as a whole life comprises the total system of Earth elements, probably leaving aside a few of them, as, e.g., *thorium*, but probably comprising all of them in the different isotopes. Life is a planetary phenomenon and predominantly determines the

---

7. The Laboratory of Biogeochemistry of the Academy of Sciences of the U.S.S.R. The italicized passages in the quoted excerpts of his paper are copied from the original of the English translation.

8. Remember, that this was written in 1935, before the work done on transuranic regions of the Periodic Table.

chemistry, and the migration of chemical elements of the upper shell of the Earth—the *biosphere*; it determines the migration of all the chemical elements. A quantitative investigation of such a migration is the fundamental task of the Laboratory."[9]

Next, consider a series of paragraphs which I have excerpted, for emphasis, from Section III of his report, and, after that, a pair of the opening paragraphs from Section IV.

"1. For life the field of life—the *biosphere*—is not a structureless casual Earth's surface—the face of the planet upon which life originated, according to E. Seuss, or the cosmic medium of life according to Cl. Bernard. The biosphere is not only the face of the Earth and not a cosmic medium. The Earth's shell has a strictly definite composition and structure, determining and controlling all the phenomena that take place within it, the phenomena of life included; it is morphologically distinct but closely related to the general structure of the planet.

"A number of the most characteristic and important geological phenomena establish such a character of the biosphere with certainty. Its chemical composition, as well as all the other features of its structure, is not casual and is most intimately related to the structure and time of the planet and determines the form of life observed."

And, next:

"The biosphere is not an amorphous nature, a structureless part of the space-time, in which biological phenomena are studied and established independently of it; it has a definite structure changing in time according to definite laws. This is to be taken into consideration in all the scientific deductions, in the logic of natural science in the first place; and this is not done. The 'nature' of the naturalist is only the biosphere. It is something very definite and delimitated."

And next:

"If this structure is called a mechanism, it would be a special, very peculiar mechanism, a continuously changing mechanism—a dynamic equilibrium—never reaching a state strictly identical in the past and in the future. At every moment of the past and of the future time the equilibrium is different but closely resembling. It contains so many components, so many parameters, so many independent variables, that no strict and precise return of some state in its previous form is possible.

An idea of it may be given by comparing it to the dynamic equilibrium of the living organism itself. In this sense it is more convenient to speak of the *organized state*, rather than of the *mechanism* of the biosphere."

And, from the first, second, and third paragraphs of III.2:

"Life is continuously and immutably connected with the biosphere. It is inseparable from the latter materially and energetically. The living organisms are connected with the biosphere through their nutrition, breathing, reproduction, metabolism. This connection may be precisely and fully expressed quantitatively by the migration of atoms from the biosphere to the living organism and back again—*the biogenic migration of atoms*. The more energetic the biogenic migration of the atoms, the more intense is life. It is nearly dying out or hardly flickering in the latest phases of life, the importance of which in the organized state has not yet been evaluated, but should not be overlooked.

"The biogenic migration of atoms compromises the whole of the biosphere and is the fundamental natural phenomenon characteristic of it.

"In the aspect of historical time—within a decamyriad, a hundred thousand years,—there is no natural phenomenon in the biosphere more geologically powerful than life."

And, under III.3, the following most relevant pair of paragraphs appears:

"The chief geological importance of these masses of substance embraced by life, that seem small when compared to the mass of the biosphere, is connected with their exclusively great energetic activity.

"This property of the living substance, having nothing equal to it in the substance of the planet, not only at the given moment, but also in the aspect of geological time, completely distinguishes it from any other earthly substance and makes the distinction between the living and inert substance of the planet quite sharp, the more so that all the living is derived from the living. The connection between the living and the inert substance of the biosphere is indissoluble and material within the geological time—of the order of a milliard of years, and is maintained exclusively by the biogenic migration of atoms. Abiogenesis is not known in any form of its manifestation. Practically, the naturalist cannot overlook in his work this empirically precise deduction from a scientific observation of nature, even if he does not agree with it due to his religious or philosophically religious premises."

---

9. Vernadsky, op. cit.

And, then, finally, the four paragraphs opening section IV:

"The whole work of the Laboratory is based on such a structure of the biosphere, on the existence of an impassable sharp, materially energetical boundary between the living and the inert substance.

"It is necessary to dwell on this point, since it appears to me that in this question there is a vagueness of thought, which impedes scientific work.

"We do not proceed here beyond exact empiric observation, the deductions from which are obligatory for the scientist and as a matter of fact for everyone; it is on this observation that he not only *can* but *must* base his work. These deductions may possibly be explained differently, but in the form of *empiric generalization* they are to be taken into consideration in science, for an empiric generalization is neither a scientific theory, nor a scientific hypothesis, nor else a working hypothesis. This generalized expression of scientifically established facts is logically as obligatory as the scientific facts themselves—if it has been logically correctly formulated.

"The sharp material energetic distinction of the living organisms in the biosphere—of the living substance of the biosphere—from any other substance of the biosphere penetrates the whole field of phenomena studied in biogeochemistry."

From that point on, Vernadsky leads the discussion into the region of a Pasteur-Curie conception, a subject of continuing importance for treating the outcome of Vernadsky's life-time work as a whole, but which should be left for discussion at some other occasion, since we must tend to bound the present discussion here within the limits of the scope of that special topic of method which I have posed to be the subject immediately at hand here.

The Significance of Those Examples

The set of excerpted passages which I have just presented, should remind us of deliberations which should have been familiar from among the most notable features of the greatest known moments of ancient through modern science, especially those highlights of the modern science set into motion by the Fifteenth-Century genius, Cardinal Nicholas of Cusa, and such of his explicitly avowed and faithful followers as Luca Pacioli, Leonardo da Vinci, and Johannes Kepler. We must continue attention to the principle expressed by those authors, to include such followers of Kepler as Fermat and Leibniz, and such followers of Leibniz as Carl Gauss, Lejeune Dirichlet, and Bernhard Riemann. The point which I am stressing in this report, is that the methodological approach expressed by the quoted passages from Vernadsky above, should remind us of Gauss's wrestling with a crucial topic of Earth magnetism, also of the related topic, which we encounter under Vernadsky's four paragraphs of his Section IV above, the topic of the development of what Riemann emphasized as Dirichlet's Principle, and also Riemann's own work based extensively on the immediate foundations developed by his own principal teachers Gauss and Dirichlet.

When this cited 1935 material on the Biosphere is taken inclusively into account, there is no reason to doubt that Vernadsky's work is, as he claims in later writings on the Noösphere, authentically Riemannian.[10]

As I have emphasized at the beginning of this report, knowledge of a discovery of principle is obtained only by experiencing the process of its discovery, not by learning recipes, nor by the deductive methods of the reductionists. *What is most significant in my pointing to the referenced excerpts from Vernadsky's 1935 report on methods of biogeochemistry, is the way in which he structures the process of discovery of that principle which separates the biosphere categorically from a part of the universe which is determined only by the principles of non-living processes.*

The same method for defining such a discovery which he describes in the indicated 1935 report, is that which I developed, in emphatic opposition to Wiener and von Neumann, for defining the underlying, anti-entropic principle of a science of physical economy. On my recent first reading of the 1935 paper at hand, I recognized immediately, that the method he sets forth in that paper for defining the domain of biogeochemistry, provides us evidence of the method he had employed for his subsequent discovery of his concept of the Noösphere, thus filling in some important evidence which I had not found explicitly provided in satisfactory degree in what I had known of translations of his writings on the Noösphere.[11]

____

10. LaRouche, op. cit.

11. As I have stressed in an earlier location, to appreciate the work of Vernadsky, one must take into account the aversive circumstances of the hostility his achievements bestirred among the official Marxist-Leninist ideologues of those times and places. The concepts which I reference, as crucial, in this present report, would be deeply resented by any reductionist ideologues, including the most zealous materialists of the F. "Opposable Thumb" Engels tradition in "science." It is only to be added,

I emphasize what I have already stated, that the principle of method expressed by Vernadsky in those cited passages corresponds to what Riemann emphasized as Dirichlet's Principle, a Principle whose footprint jumps up at me in the series of passages from Vernadsky's 1935 document which I have excerpted above. The use of the same method from the 1935 paper, when applied to the subject of the specific distinctions of human behavior from anything met in other living processes, defines the *noëtic* principle of human cognition as distinct from anything otherwise found in the domain of the biosphere.

I emphasize to the present reader, that I am writing this at a time when some of my associates among the LaRouche Youth Movement (LYM) have relived the process of discovery of Riemannian physical geometry to the degree that they have had notable successes in treating some of the essential content of Bernard Riemann's 1857 Theory of Abelian Functions. That is the work by Riemann in which his employ of what he terms Dirichlet's Principle plays a pervasive role. The report I am delivering here, is intended, inclusively, to provoke those readers into developing some useful supplementary insights into the implications of the role of the Dirichlet Principle in Riemann's advanced work. Obviously, once that special part of my intended audience is taken into account, what I present here is relevant for a still broader audience.

1. The Matter of Sphaerics

The method of investigation which Vernadsky expresses in the cited 1935 paper is in the same "archeological" tradition as that which the ancient Thales and the Pythagoreans adopted as the Egyptian school of astrophysical science known to the Greeks as "Sphaerics."

For example, the term "archeology" is perhaps the best choice of irony for pointing to the need to consider the fact of a turbulent transition which occurred after perhaps something less than 10,000 years of initial melting of the hundreds of thousands of years of glaciation of much of the northern continental hemisphere, during an interval prior to the climactic melting which flooded a great fresh-water lake, now known as the Black Sea, with the salt water flooded in from the Atlantic by way of the Mediterranean.[12] *I now emphasize a special kind of archeology, not usually treated as such, in which a lack of material available on site must be overcome by focusing on what early periods of human existence and development, which, perhaps, occurred in other places, must have deposited as ideas, as if these were footprints, on the physical archeological site whose evidence we are considering.*

After all, the human species, as distinguished from apes and other animals by the human individual's cognitive powers, has lived on this planet for as long as perhaps a million years, or, perhaps, even much more. The transmission of the cognitive kinds of ideas which are unique to, and everywhere characteristic of the behavior of the human species, must have been transmitted, in significant part, into historical times and places from very ancient dates, and from different places, certainly long, long before 17,000 B.C., including the hundreds of thousands of preceding years of generations, during a time much of the northern hemisphere was under great slabs of glacial ice.

Despite the kinds of great "natural" catastrophes, and also man-made relative dark ages which mankind has endured on this planet, there is a wonderfully stubborn resilience of our species, such that something essential springs up from the ashes of catastrophe, sometimes transmitted from earlier places where human habitation may have been subsequently erased.

Thus, ideas such as those expressed by the Egypt of the time of the building of the Great Pyramids, must have been largely developed in other places, from a time when the levels of the oceans were about four hundred feet lower than today, a time even tens of thousands of years prior to the first settlements near the mouth of the Nile of that time, and prior to the changes in climate and geography of our planet brought about by the melting of the earlier great glaciation.

We are looking therefore, from sites such as ancient Egypt, into much earlier, glacial times during which the most advanced cultures of the world were transoceanic, and, as some of Bal Gangadhar Tilak's relevant works point out,[13] the most advanced knowledge was dominated by the role of astronomy in such prominently included functions as astrogation. The very long astronomical cycles referenced by the work on ancient

---

that the Marxist-Leninists were comparatively innocents on this account, when compared with the virtual criminality of our contemporary positivist and existentialist tribes.

12. E.g., Plato, *Timaeus*, passim.

13. *Orion, Arctic Home in the Vedas.*

calendars of Tilak and others, and study of the methods employed by Thales, Aristarchus of Samos, Eratosthenes, and others, shows us how such knowledge of astronomy and astrogation was developed by methods implicitly available to any ancient civilization, even of the glacial ages, by cultures which were engaged by the challenge of transoceanic astrogation.[14]

Mankind's earlier attributable science, in the sense of modern physical science, framed man's concept of that which is universal, by looking upward toward the universe in the large. It is definite knowledge, that the birth of science in European civilization, such as the work of Thales and the Pythagoreans, was principally influenced from Egyptian sources falling under the category of *Sphaerics,* not the contrary, reductionist methods typical of Mesopotamia, for example. As the work of Vernadsky in the matters of the Biosphere and Noösphere should remind us, it is Egyptian Sphaerics which supplied European civilization with its original science, its original notion of science as subsumed by those purely physical-geometrical notions of universality which man recognizes in the astrophysical depths of an Egyptian astronomy which had turned, long before the time of the Pythagoreans, to the long waves of development of astrophysics which were continued into the work of the Eratosthenes whose discoveries made possible the map, crafted by Toscanelli, and used by Christopher Columbus to guide his first voyage of Transatlantic discovery.

The greatest, and most ancient of all archeological artefacts, are to be found in the domains of astrophysics and its application to such subjects as transoceanic navigation.[15]

If we can fairly estimate the local origins of Egyptian culture as dating from approximately 8,000 B.C., how might the culture reflected in the astrophysical characteristics of the Great Pyramids be traced to roots in the forms of human civilized existence existing under the conditions of glaciation? Implicitly, that is the issue of scientific method which permeates Vernadsky's 1935 design for the further scientific work of his Laboratory in fundamental questions of biogeochemistry. Such were the methods of *Sphaerics* employed by the Pythagoreans and their follower Plato.

What is human about the Great Pyramids of Egypt, for example? Is it the stones? Or, is it not something modern man was often reluctant to discover, the ideas expressed in the way those stones were arranged, and in the methods by which those pyramids were constructed? It is tens of thousands of years of astronomy expressed by the physical principles which those stones express, as we see, similarly, the implications of the Equinoctial cycle expressed by the calendars embedded in Vedic hymns composed in Central Asia more than six thousand years ago.

The way in which the human mind, working in societies over intervals of many generations, generates valid ideas respecting the practicable knowledge of the organization of the processes of our planet, is as much an archeological artefact as any physical object or written ancient record. This is the case, even if the place where this idea was developed no longer exists to provide us a physical record of that culture's activity. Rather, because of the nature of man, as distinct from the beasts, those ideas are much more the characteristic physical, archeological expression, the truer artefact of humanity, than any mere physical artefacts in themselves.

A practicable applied science of the way in which the *noëtic* power specific to the human mind develops discoveries of principles and of their applications, should be adopted as the most important of all working archeological principles. This has reflections in Vernadsky's treatment of the geology of the Biosphere in the 1935 paper, and is the implied challenge for the development of an applied archeology (i.e., epistemology) of the cognitive domain of human existence.

On this account, the notable characteristic distinction of the work within the domain of *Sphaerics* by the Pythagoreans and Plato, is that it belongs within the category of astrophysics, rather than the mere astronomy of an Aristotelean such as the celebrated Roman

---

14. There is a reflection, thus, from distantly ancient times in the work bearing on even "ice age" cultures by the Egyptian Platonic Academy representative of Cyrenaic origin, Eratosthenes. His measurement of the longitudinal circumference of the Earth, from within Egypt, and his measurement of the distance along the arc from Alexandria to Rome, are exemplary. Compare this with Tilak's **Orion** and **Arctic Home in the Vedas**.

15. A notable precedent is to be found, once again, in the way in which Toscanelli, a close collaborator of Cardinal Nicholas of Cusa, crafted the map of the world which was used by Christopher Columbus to rediscover North America. Despite Venetian lies respecting the distance from Italy to the coast of China, the principles expressed by the crafting of that map are to be traced to the work of the Platonic Academy's Eratosthenes, who measured the longitudinal circumference of the Earth from two points within ancient Egypt. Similar is the case emphasized by Tilak in his **Orion**, of the knowledge of the equinoctial astronomical cycle by a Vedic culture existing in central Asia during the interval 6,000-4,000 B.C.

Imperial hoaxster Claudius Ptolemy, or the more honorable later astronomers such as Copernicus and Tycho Brahe. This distinction of ancient astrophysics from ancient and modern astronomy as such, is best presented today from the vantage-point of Carl Gauss's crucial 1799 attack on the hoaxes perpetrated by empiricist fanatics such as D'Alembert, Euler, and Lagrange—fanatics imitated by Laplace and Cauchy later. As Gauss made explicit in his later writings on the subject of The Fundamental Theorem of Algebra, the relevant distinction between mere astronomy and astrophysics, as applied retrospectively to the case of the Pythagoreans, is expressed in modern mathematical-physics language as the Gauss-Riemann notion of a physics, rather than a mere mathematics, of the complex domain. This mathematical-physical, rather than merely formal-mathematical view of the complex domain, is indispensable for insight into the powerful implications of Vernadsky's discoveries.

The evidence which qualifies us to say that one ape-like creature is human, and another essentially represents some species of ape, is that characteristic of the human mind which is the well-spring of mankind's ability to effect willful increases of our species' potential relative population-density. The distinction is not, as we know, "tool-making," for which even chimpanzees created in the likeness claimed by F. Engels have shown aptitude. It is creative behavior of the type expressed by the discovery and proof of some universal physical principle. *It is such creative behavior which distinguishes mankind systemically, as the conception of the Biosphere reflected in the quotations introduced above distinguishes living from abiotic processes.*

Let us emphasize this point. This quality of behavior, unique to the human species, is not found in biology, just as Vernadsky emphasized, the principle of life is nowhere found within the ontological bounds of the abiotic domain.

Therefore, in the study of living species we do not define life as a phenomenon of the inorganic laboratory, but only as Vernadsky does, in terms of effects which could not be produced by an abiotic physics. *Life is produced only by life.* Cognition is generated, not as a characteristic of living processes, but as the characteristic impact of the respectively higher principle of cognition upon living processes.

Therefore, the method employed by Vernadsky is the method of systemic studies of fossils. We compare the fossils of abiotic activity with the contrasted fossils of living activity, and contrast the cognitive processes to the fossils of non-human living activity. *Only cognition can produce a cognitive response.* It is the artefacts of cognition which express humanity. It is the fossils of cognitive action which betray the evidence of the existence and character of the human species. Every categorical kind of distinction which Vernadsky cites, as in the sample of excerpts from his 1935 paper, has a parallel in distinguishing the content of the Noösphere from that of the Biosphere.

Thus, the difference between the human species and other living entities, lies in the difference in ordering of their accumulation of fossils. We can not see life in the physics of abiotic processes. We can not see cognition, the distinction of the human individual from the beast, in the living matter of the human individual. We see cognition in its artefacts, the artefacts of those creative powers of the individual human mind which can not be found within the bounds of biology. In the Biosphere, we see the power of life manifest in the ongoing ordering of fossils. In the Noösphere, we see, as the relevant class of "fossils," the effects of the noëtic powers of the mind of the individual member of the human species.

In the fossils of the Biosphere, we trace the shadow of the hand of life. In the fossils of the Noösphere, we trace the shadow of the hand of cognition, of the noëtic principle of the sovereignly individual mind.

Look at the physical principle of the complex domain, as made adequately clear by the combination of Riemann's 1854 habilitation dissertation and 1857 Theory of Abelian Functions, in that light.

Geistesmasse and Dirichlet's Principle

The notion of the complex domain was a necessary development of mathematics, in order to free mathematics from formal mathematics' perversion, from its enslavement by a reductionist's system of an *a priori* set of so-called definitions, axioms, and postulates. It was Riemann's use of this work by Carl Gauss, to free science from the numbing of the human mind by allegedly "self-evident" definitions, axioms, and postulates, as Riemann did in his 1854 habilitation dissertation; it was Riemann's continuation of that development, strengthened by a legacy of the work of Abel and Dirichlet, which made possible the development of a form of physical science which were uncorrupted by aprioristic or other reductionist presumptions. For this later accomplishment, as by Riemann, the work of Leibniz and Gauss, and of Cusa, Leonardo, and Kepler before Fermat and Leibniz, were among the most crucial modern precedents.

The reductionist's foolish, blind faith in the alleged self-evidence of sense-perceptual experience, depends upon ignoring the elementary fact, that sense-experience is not reality *per se*, but, rather, merely the conscious reflection by the senses, of the impact of some aspects of physical reality upon them. Within the bounds of a mathematics based strictly upon sense-perception-oriented, reductionist views, such as those of a classroom Euclidean geometry, there is no place allowed for the experimentally demonstrated existence of an efficient form of universal physical principle. This problem of representation was solved, largely through the work of Gauss's laying the groundwork for the physical conception of a complex domain. However, the principle expressed by Gauss et al. in this way, was already implicit in the view of *Sphaerics* expressed by the work of the Pythagoreans, and by Plato after them.

Experimentally validatable sense perceptions are real, but are not reality as such. Reality is expressed, typically, by notions such as *life* and *cognition*, two really efficient classes of states of the physical universe, whose effects are efficiently expressed as the experience of our senses, *but which are not themselves the explicit subjects of sense-perception.* We know these so-called transcendent realities, such as life and cognition, only in a way which the notion of the Gauss-Riemann complex domain reflects. Dirichlet's Principle was recognized by Riemann as the necessary ontological glue which made the connection between the two aspects of the complex function truly comprehensible. We recognize these realities in the only way in which they could be recognized, by the successful practice of living beings in general, as known through the application of the creative mental powers unique to the human species.

When the chief work of Vernadsky is considered from this historical vantage-point in science, his successive definitions of Biosphere (life) and Noösphere (cognition), the deepest experimental implications of Riemann's insight into Dirichlet's Principle, and the related implications of Riemann's emphasis upon *Geistesmasse,* are made clearer from an experimental standpoint.[16]

____
16. Cf. ***Bernhard Riemanns Gesammelte Mathematische Werke***, H. Weber, ed. (New York: Dover Publications reprint edition, 1953). See Riemann's posthumously published papers in that location. *Geistesmasse* can be roughly translated as "thought object."

The Dirichlet Principle

In his 1857 essay *Theory of Abelian Functions,* Bernhard Riemann brought to light the deeper epistemological significance of the complex domain, through a new and bold application of a principle of physical action which he called "Dirichlet's Principle." Riemann's approach, combined with what he enunciated in his habilitation dissertation of 1854, ushered in a revolution in scientific thinking.

Lejeune Dirichlet was a pivotal figure in early 19th Century science, in the tradition of Carl Friedrich Gauss. Riemann studied with Dirichlet beginning in 1847, and when Dirichlet died in 1859, Riemann was appointed to his chair at Göttingen University.

For further elaboration, see:

"Bernhard Riemann's 'Dirichlet Principle,'" by Bruce Director.

"LeJeune Dirichlet and the Mendelssohn Youth Movement," by David Shavin.

I shall explain this, but, that I might do so, first, permit me to resume my attention to what I shall show to be the historical matter of *Sphaerics.*

Sphaerics, as the Pythagoreans and Plato used it, signifies *universality.* Experience shows that we on Earth dwell within a deep universe whose most typical expression for the senses, is motions apparently ordered for our sense-perceptions as within a spherical experience of the universe we observe from the surface of our home planet. It is perceived as a spherical form of physical space-time of unknown, but vast depth.

Within this there are certain observed motions which, when normalized to take into account the motions of the Earth itself, are simply circular or spherical: the universe according to the doctrine of Aristotle, for example, the universe of mere astronomy.

Then, there are seemingly anomalous astronomical

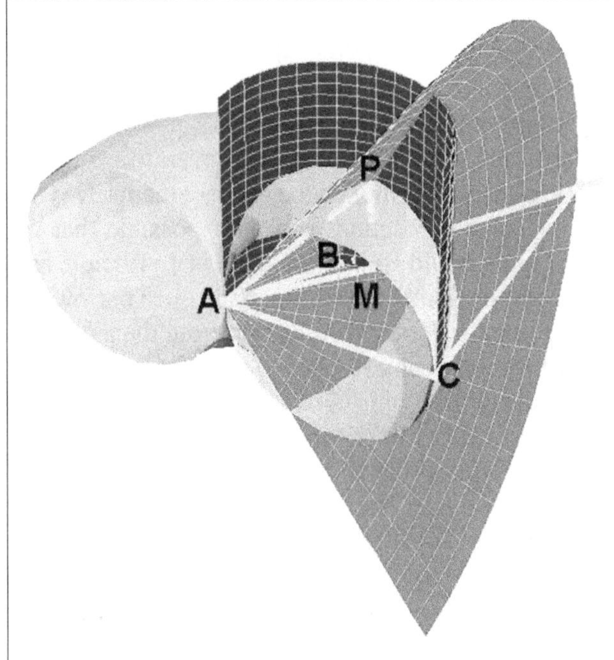

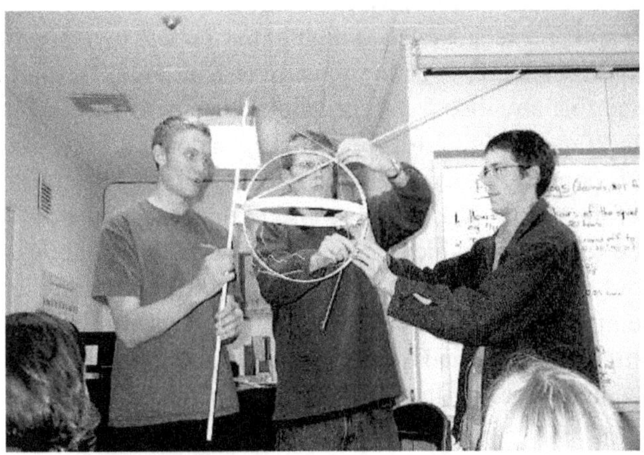

Archytas' solution to the Delian paradox typifies the work of pre-Euclidean, physical, constructive geometry. Here, members of the LaRouche Youth Movement have built a pedagogical device to demonstrate his solution, which creates a cone, a torus, and a cylinder in order to find the geometric means between two magnitudes—AC and AB in the drawing For animated graphics of this and related problems in constructive geometry, see Lyndon H. LaRouche, Jr., "Our Economic Policy: Animation and Economics," at www.larouchepac.com.

motions which do not fit such simplistic explanations; there are higher forms of regularity which express unseen, but efficient universal physical principles acting within and upon the apparently astronomical universe. These higher forms of regularity, in which universal physical principles are defined, is the domain

of astrophysics. This defines the essential difference between Copernicus and Kepler, the essential superiority of the work of Kepler over that of Copernicus and Brahe, the difference between mere astronomy and astrophysics.

As the application of knowledge of thermonuclear fusion compels us to view Kepler's organization of the Solar System accordingly, all Earth-bound physical science becomes a subsumed feature of astrophysics. Astrophysics is, thus, the context in which all competent pursuit of physical science must be located, and from which the most crucial aspects of physical science, such as those traced from Thales, the Pythagoreans, et al. to ancient Egypt, must be traced.

The case of the Pythagorean Archytas' construction of the doubling of the cube solely by geometrical methods, is, thus, the prime example of the principle of astrophysics passed down from the Pythagoreans, through Plato's scientific method, to the present. The relevance of Archytas' solution for the constructive exact doubling of the cube, is the relevant provocation leading through Gauss's 1799 attack on the fanatical blunders of D'Alembert, Euler, and Lagrange, to the level of development of physical science associated with the life's work of Riemann. This astrophysical principle is the key to that aspect of the organization of Vernadsky's mind expressed in his approach to defining both the Biosphere and Noösphere. The outline of the adopted tasks set forth in the referenced 1935 paper, is typical of this method.

In the experience represented by the Gaussian complex domain, we combine the notion of the sensed object with the notion of the effect on its motion generated by the unsensed, but efficiently manifested principle. One component is, on principle, a view of the relevant phenomenon within the domain of a spherical universal space-time of sense-experience. The other component is the unseen, but actual universal physical principles acting upon the object of perception. The modern typification of this relationship is the argument underlying Cusa follower Kepler's uniquely original discovery of a principle of universal gravitation, a discovery which marks the modern transformation of mere astronomy into a subject of astrophysics. After that, no longer can motion within the observed universe be attributed to the repeatable regularity of motion, as by the modern defenders of the hoaxster Claudius Ptolemy, but must be traced to the power exerted by an unseen, but efficient and knowable universal physical principle.

When we trace the intellectual history of the idea of

the complex domain from the practice of *Sphaerics* by the Pythagoreans and Plato, we proceed in mathematical constructions through the anti-Euclidean, geometrical doubling of the square, to Archytas' geometrical doubling of the cube. The implications of this are made clearer through recognition of the frauds which the Leibniz-hating empiricist ideologues, D'Alembert, Euler, and Euler's protégé Lagrange perpetrated in connection with existence of those cubic roots which are, in fact, implicitly locatable within Archytas' construction. The situating of the implications, for experimental *Sphaerics*, of elliptical and higher functions implicit in Kepler's uniquely original discovery of gravitation, and related discovery of the harmonic ordering of planetary orbits, defines the needs to go beyond the barest conception of *Sphaerics,* as a precondition for mathematical conceptualization of the existence of any universal physical principle.

So, Kepler summarized this and his related accomplishments in study of the Solar System as a whole, with two directives transmitted as tasks to "future mathematicians." First, the development of a truly infinitesimal calculus, that of the type uniquely developed by Gottfried Leibniz, including Leibniz's catenary-cued, universal physical principle of least action. Second, the importance of the generalization of the implications of elliptical functions shown not only in the characteristic of Earth's orbit, but the composition of the Solar System in general. The latter work was accomplished by contributions from numerous contemporaries of Gauss, chiefly French and German, but especially by Gauss and Riemann. This was the framework for the general development of the notions of the complex domain, and of curvature, by Gauss, and the continuation of Gauss's work by the original discoveries of Riemann.

Yet, we must never lose sight of the fact, that these accomplishments of modern European science are rooted in the Pythagoreans' and Plato's development of the Egyptian heritage of *Sphaerics*. Progress was never simply continuous in history. The emergence of reductionists such as the Eleatics, the materialists, the Sophists, the Aristoteleans, and the Romans, were grave intellectual and moral set-backs to the progress of European civilization. From the historical vantage-point presented by that view of history, the ideas of the Pythagoreans were not actually superseded by the development of those reductionist systems which repudiated the original Pythagorean-Platonic basis. The essential axiomatic issues posed to the Pythagoreans are still among the most crucial issues for scientific method today.

The crux of all ontological issues so posed by the known history of civilization, European civilization in only its specific way, may be stated as a question: "Since universal physical principles are proven to exist with full efficiency, even though they are not themselves objects of sense-perception, how is it possible that the human mind could conceive a universal principle as a object of the mind? For this, Riemann once borrowed a concept for such objects of thought from the anti-Kantian educational philosopher Herbart, *Geistesmasse*. Later, he expressed this notion by reference to what he identified as Dirichlet's Principle, with notable emphasis on the implications of his own 1857 ***The Theory of Abelian Functions***, the theory of the generalized *Riemann Surface*. Vernadsky's definition of the methods of investigation of the Biosphere, and his concept of the Noösphere, are conceptions of this type associated with Riemann's notion of Dirichlet's Principle.

Any validatable physical principle is universal in its intent and scope, even though it may appear to apply to special situations within the universe at large. We may say that any discovered principle appears to have been lurking, waiting for its opportunity to pounce. How can we conceive of a universal principle as a definite object of the mind? A useful response to that question would be the way in which Riemann replaced (but doubtless did not discard) his use of the term *Geistesmasse* by his emphasis on Dirichlet's Principle. We hear little explicitly from Riemann on the subject of *Geistesmasse* again, because the mathematical-physical technical term for that named subject was changed to *Dirichlet's Principle*.

Dirichlet's Principle defines a class of physically efficient mental objects which are never perceived, but whose existence is efficiently demonstrated by crucial types of experiments. *Life* and *Cognition* are higher qualities of expression of such objects.

These objects do not exist as real in the vocabulary of the relatively stupefied intellects of the class known to theologians as *Gnostics*, such as reductionists, such as the materialists, empiricists, positivists, existentialists, and as killers in the names of religion, of the type of Dostoevsky's Grand Inquisitor, who may say "Kill them all and let God sort them out."

That much said, let us proceed by taking the further discussion of this subject to my own home-base, the subject of the science of physical economy.

2. The Science of Physical Economy

The same quality of conceptual challenge posed by Vernadsky's 1935 case for the biogeochemical domain, arises as the qualitatively more profound, central feature of organization presented to us by the subject-matter of economic science. This fact should not be a surprise to any matured thinking person of modern times. Cognition is of a higher order than the abiotic and biotic domains.

It is already implicit in what is written in preceding portions of this present report, that I place the authority of the evidence of a science of physical economy, on the highest level among branches of science. The basis for making that argument is implied in Vernadsky's achievements in defining the Biosphere and Noösphere successively. As I shall restate the case at suitable points later in this present writing, the functional characteristics of the living practice of a well-defined science of physical economy, are the summation of man's capacity for acquiring and proving any kind of new experimental knowledge. It is in observations and experiments conducted from the advantageous position of that pinnacle of man's place in the universe, his place in the Noösphere, that the highest level of knowledge of physical science knowable for man is to be found.

The reader should bear that point in mind, both in reflections on what I have said respecting science above, and what I shall add below.

After all, man is a living organism, whose existence is biologically a part of the Biosphere, and depends upon the Biosphere. Yet, that is not the essential distinction of the human species, nor of the individual member of that species. The essential distinction is "intellectual," a quality in the image of the Creator of the universe, a quality of a higher order than anything experienced in any other living species. Since, as Vernadsky emphasizes, the Noösphere is expanding, relative to the Biosphere, so, just as the Biosphere should be continuing to grow relative to Earth's immediate abiotic domain, we must say that, just as Vernadsky emphasizes that abiotic material is used by the processes of the Biosphere, and exchanged within the abiotic domain, so the biotic features of the human individual, and individuals are used in accord with those higher principles expressed in the Noösphere.

Mankind's historically recent personal entry into exploration of nearby Solar space implies the Noösphere's absorption of the Solar System as of the Earth itself.

These considerations just stated here, are not mere analogies, but appropriate descriptions of the state of affairs already in progress.

Therefore, economy, insofar as it is not expressed in forms of mass human behavior which degrade human beings to the relatively "zero growth" population potential of a species of ape, is an expression of the highest order in the universe explicitly known to us, the Noösphere. Therefore, no one should be astonished to learn that any competent theory of economy must have the most essentially distinguishing characteristics which are to be inherited, so to speak, from knowledge of the participating role of the principles distinguishing both the respective and combined characteristics of the Biosphere and Noösphere. In other words, the same kinds of qualifications which Vernadsky's 1935 work specifies for the Biosphere's distinction from the abiotic domain, and, similarly, for the distinction of the Noösphere from the Biosphere, are the implicit foundations of any competent approach to defining and governing a real modern economy.

In the simplest kind of example of the discovery of a universal physical principle, the apparatus, or its functional equivalent employed by us, contains a feature which corresponds to the demonstration of the principle which is being tested. This is typified by the crafting of machine-tool designs for such purposes as testing an hypothetical experimental principle. If the test experiment has a positive outcome, the relevant aspect of the machine-tool or like experimental design, then becomes the point of departure for designing processes, such as those which might be used in manufacturing, processes which incorporate the function of the discovered principle into regular human practice.

I have often used the image of the "goldfish bowl" to illustrate the significance of this kind of experience. This consideration brings us to the point of reflections on a crucial problem of economy considered as a physical, rather than a monetary process.

In contemporary societies so far, most of the people operate on the basis of a set of the typical individual's more or less witting assumptions, some of which are supported by practice, and many frankly absurd. The total set of such assumptions, useful and false combined, is a mind-set which can be likened to the condition of a captive fish in a fishbowl-like container. So, it might often appear to us that the behavior of those people we observe in action is confined within virtual walls, like those of some container, where no such "wall" actually exists outside their own mind. Those people are not responding to the real world; they are confining their actions to a special, imagined world, whose "walls" are not only a combination of both respectable and absurd axiomatic assumptions alike, but also reflect much ignorance of and indifference to many actual principles and conditions existing in the universe.

The simplest classroom illustration of this can be provided by showing the pathological character of the set of definitions, axioms, and postulates associated with a classroom Euclidean or Cartesian geometry. This presents us with a case in which all of these varieties of presumptions are false. Constructions made according to those principles of *Sphaerics* employed by the Pythagoreans and by Plato, lead us toward direct and accurate calculations, whereas attempts to address the same matter within the framework of a Euclidean or Cartesian geometry become a cause for rituals which incur needless frustrations, and often also embarrassing mistakes.[17]

We must concede, however, that the ideal Euclidean or Cartesian mind, while inherently pathological in its own right, might seem to be almost a marvel of orderliness, even a certain excellence, when it is compared with the currently prevalent everyday opinions of most people on the subject of scientific and social behavior in general. No further concession in this matter were needed, or permissible.

In any case, the elimination of false, axiom-like assumptions, or the addition of a discovered, valid universal principle, has an effect which causes the range of behavior to extend into a realm outside the implied walls of that person's prior, goldfish-bowl-like belief-system. The effect of such changes is to raise the power of the relevant human activity by some order of magnitude.

Thus, for example, the increase of the density of power expressed by technological progress from sunlight, to wood-burning, to charcoal, to coal and coke, to nuclear, and to thermonuclear power, represents a kind of effect which we may interpret as human willful increases in the intensity of heat per square meter of cross-section of the relevant heat-flow. My associates and I have often found it convenient to present this fact in the language of "energy-flux density." These and related increases of the density of the equivalent of heat-flow are marked by points at which a qualitative change in society's relationship to its environment occurs, a change from a relatively less powerful, to a more powerful system.

Usually, it is the intensity of the heat-flow, rather than the total amount of heat added, which defines the crucial points in this process. Thus, proceeding from various forms of chemical combustion as a source of heat, to nuclear fission, and then thermonuclear fusion, corresponds to a shift to qualitatively higher forms of physical action. The critical values marked along a scale of such changes, each correspond to successively higher physical states, such that mankind's power over its environment, per capita, and per square kilometer, is increased qualitatively at critical points of qualitative change.

Generally, these qualitative improvements in man's power to exist, are the outgrowth of either discarding some of what are shown to have been false "axiomatic-like" assumptions, or the addition of the use of a discovered new principle, or some combination of both types of actions. This means either "tearing down the walls" of the fishbowl, or moving the walls outward, to encompass more and more of the real universe in mankind's search for a greater scope for the quality of action which is relevant to the increase of, and capacity for survival of the human species. Different categories of what we may measure by the crude yardstick, "energy," may be regarded as presenting us with "walls" which can be breached only through qualitative changes in scope of human practice.

Notably, the principal markers of the qualitative implications of these increases of intensity may be either molecular (distinguishing both abiotic and biotic), atomic, nuclear (e.g., nuclear fission), or sub-nuclear (thermonuclear, matter-antimatter). The quality of action possible, and the order of nature in which the domains for such qualities of action are entered, compel us to give up simplistic ideas about "energy,"[18] and to

---

17. For example, the assumption of three respectively independent senses of direction in empty space depends, as Euler, in his own 1761 **Letters to a German Princess**, argues against Leibniz in his insistence upon a value of "absolute zero" curvature for any interval of action, whereas experimental physics, such as those of Leibniz's universal physical principle of least action, shows that, contrary to Euler, Lagrange, and Cauchy, for example, no infinitesimal could be so small that it would have "zero" curvature. There is no existing abstract space, time, or matter, but only efficient physical space-time. The absurdity of Euclidean and Cartesian reductionist schemes is about the only thing in geometry which is truly self-evident.

18. The fact that we can measure the height of dogs, cows, and people by the same yardstick, does not allow us to class all as species of yardsticks.

regard today's popular beliefs about "energy" not as expressing the work of nature, but as the product of superstitions crafted in service of fallible ideologies.

The discovery of practicable approaches to controllable use of resources of these relatively higher order domains, is one of the ways in which walls of the ideological fishbowl of current cultural practice are to be broken.

The willful changes in behavior, in organization and use of power, by means of which mankind maintains and also increases our species' potential relative population-density, express a unique distinction of the human species from all lower forms of life, including, of course, each and all of the varieties of great apes. The resulting distinction of man from the lower forms of life, defines an implied argument which sets man's existence essentially above the Biosphere within which he participates. That is so in the sense, for Vernadsky's 1935 paper, that the principle of life distinguishes the concert of living processes from the abiotic domain. *This distinction is an essential universal principle of real economies.*

What is true of raising the level of the quality of power applied, is paralleled by other adoptions of valid added principles to the repertoire of human action.

So, just as the principle expressed by living processes defines a boundary separating the Biosphere from the abiotic domain, so the effect of the principle of cognition defines a Noösphere which is functionally and otherwise distinct from the Biosphere. The three domains, the abiotic, the Biosphere, and the Noösphere, interact, and exchange material with one another, but, as Vernadsky argues in the 1935 location referenced here, the boundary which separates the one process from the others is definite, and of the quality of a lawful universal physical principle. The appropriate conception of such boundaries is the notion of Dirichlet's Principle.

There is not one of the conditions I have selected from what is described by Vernadsky, in the 1935 report, for this kind of distinction of the Biosphere from the abiotic domain, which does not have a correlative in the distinction of the Noösphere—*which is to say the physical economy*—from both the abiotic and the Biosphere, although it is the same abiotic and organic material of the universe at large which is shared among them. The three systems, abiotic, Biosphere, and Noösphere, each have a characteristic universal principle of action, distinct from the other two. In each case, action within that domain is organized according to that characteristic principle of the domain, but the principles typical of each domain, and therefore the result, are different.

However, although it is correct to emphasize the relative distinction of each of the domains from the others, there are higher principles which both define the commonality of the elements of that three-fold domain, and also order the relations among them.[19] This brings us to the challenge represented by the idea of human cognition itself. After treating cognition as creation, I shall return our attention to the matter of the comparison of the ways in which Vernadsky and I have, respectively, obliged ourselves to treat the issues of universal principle associated with the respective phenomena of life and cognition.

What Is, and What Is Not Creation?

The human discovery and use of a discovered universal physical principle, is not only an efficiently physical action. It is one of the essential expressions of the most typical quality of categorically human activity. To follow Vernadsky: *It defines the way in which society (i.e., the Noösphere) organizes the flow of both abiotic and organic materials which it absorbs, uses, and discharges.*

At this point, I must illustrate that point in ways which engage what might be termed the practical experience of economy by any intelligent citizen.

The individual thinks of a useful sort of typical product of agriculture or manufacturing as an independent object, produced by the will of a definite set of people performing the appropriate actions in some definite place. Typically, this produced object may be transferred to some other location, where it might be stored for a while, or purchased, and taken away for consumption.

That individual thinks of the exchange of the product or service produced by one person, for a different product or service by another. Typically, it seems to each that all this can be explained in the language used for financial accounting practice. That kind of belief in accounting is essentially an illusion.

The relationship of the particular product or act of production within an economy, to the economy as a whole, is of a character more than merely analogous to the relationship among all of the components of the Biosphere to one another, and to the abiotic domain.

---

19. This kind of distinction corresponds to a notion which Plato addressed, famously, under the topic of the general notion of hypothesis.

As Vernadsky emphasized in his published 1935 work principally referenced here, the characteristic feature of the Biosphere as a whole is its development as a whole, a development from a relatively lesser, to a relatively greater significance for our planet, and, implicitly, therefore, the universe as a whole. This development, when it occurs, is characteristically anti-entropic. By anti-entropic I mean a system which is overall, characteristically anti-entropic, expressing a universal principle of action which is moving its universality as a process from lower to higher states of organization. It does not signify "negative entropy," as a case of local, temporary reversal of a universal entropy.

Thus, life is characteristically anti-entropic.

In the case of society, the directed process of increase of the Noösphere, is also characteristically anti-entropic. Absolutely or relatively entropic states may exist within part, or the whole of the Biosphere, or Noösphere at times, but such conditions are inherently pathological states of those phase-spaces.

To restate the same point, say that humanity is typically Promethean, in the sense of that term associated with Aeschylus' **Prometheus Bound**. Recall, that the evil Olympian Zeus condemned the immortal Prometheus to nearly eternal torture for imparting knowledge of the use of fire to human beings.

In other words, Zeus, like the Physiocrat Dr. François Quesnay, and Turgot later, degraded man as Quesnay based his doctrine of *laissez-faire* on the assumption that farmers were, functionally, merely a form of cattle on the titled landlord's estate. Remember that the entire economic dogma of Lord Shelburne's Anglo-Dutch Liberal system was based on the doctrine of "free trade" which Shelburne's lackey Adam Smith plagiarized from the *laissez-faire* dogma of Quesnay and Turgot. Similarly, Bernard Mandeville, the titled "patron saint" of today's Hellish Mont Pelerin Society, based the profit of society on the unbridled license of Enron-like private vice.

In reality, contrary to the Olympian Zeus, man and woman made in the image of the Creator, are naturally creative. Scientific progress based upon the realized effects of the endless discovery and command over universal physical principles, is the essential nature of mankind, the essential nature of the Noösphere. So, as evolution of species of life drives the Earth to higher states of existence, above the abiotic, so the characteristic form of successful action by society is the increase of man's power over the planet, per capita and per square kilometer of the planet's surface. This creative activity, which modern society has recognized in the benefits of scientific and technological progress, is essentially anti-entropic.

This brings us to a crucial point in the relevant argument. Since the characteristic activity which defines the existence and persistence of the Noösphere is *universal anti-entropy, the characteristic feature of every action within the Noösphere is its relative anti-entropy*. The essential part of what is being exchanged within the economic process as a whole is the relative anti-entropy expressed by the way in which the generation, circulation, and consumption of products is organized.

In this respect, the characteristics of the Biosphere, as Vernadsky and his Laboratory defined it, and Noösphere, as I define physical economies as wholes, are analogous. Everything to which I have referred, on this account, in excerpting Vernadsky's 1935 paper, has a parallel in my methods of a science of physical economy. The relations among the products of the Noösphere have an echo in the relations among the chemical elements circulating within the Biosphere, as in Vernadsky's 1935 account of such kinds of relations between the Biosphere and abiotic domain.

Both domains, the Biosphere and Noösphere, are characteristically anti-entropic, but the characteristics differ qualitatively.

Globalization as a Form of Evil

In its broader expression, creativity is expressed by Classical modes of artistic composition (as distinct from most of today's leading preferences in popular art) in plastic and non-plastic art-forms and their application to other aspects of human practice. Creativity is not something optional in human choices of behavior; that is the only thing which actually distinguishes your choice of political candidate, or painter or musician, from the apes.

It is through that action of the individual human mind, that the repertoire of increased numbers of universal physical principles are not only discovered, but deployed to change man's relationship to the universe qualitatively in an upward direction. *The increase of the Noösphere, relative to both the abiotic domain and the Biosphere, through the fruits of willful cognition, is not only a change in mankind's relationship to the universe; it is an efficient change in the characteristics of action within that universe.* Just as the Biosphere, including its fossil products, are taking over more and more of the

Earth, so the accumulation of scientific and technological progress gained through cognition of individual souls, is increasing its domination of the planet relative to the Biosphere.

I had the occasion recently to point out a certain absurdity permeating commonplace beliefs respecting so-called "globalization." That discussion occupies a notably relevant place at this point in my report. It illustrates the point which I have just made on the subject of creativity.

The suggestible, more poorly educated mind thinks of economy as the devotees of Bernard Mandeville, Adam Smith, and the British Foreign Office's Jeremy Bentham did. In fact, contrary to today's more or less conventional, and reigning "monetarist" opinion, it is a rule of thumb in modern economy that approximately half of the true cost, of the indispensable total product of labor within society, is expressed as what we term basic economic infrastructure. As we see in the still continued great margin of poverty among nearly three-quarters of the populations of leading nations with advanced agro-industrial technologies, such as China and India, the want of sufficient elaboration and distribution of truly modern forms of infrastructure expressing modern technology, makes a mockery of the search for less costly goods by runaway U.S. and European investors in what is currently called "globalization."

In such cases, we must see the lower prices of goods produced in those nations as the cause of the terrible misery within as much as seventy percent of the population as a whole. The misery is chiefly a reflection of the long-term failure to pay, and to be able to pay the necessary price of the goods produced at cheaper prices by cheaper labor.

This is reflected in the terrible degree of collapse of the internal economies of the U.S.A., Europe, and others under the so-called "floating-exchange-rate" monetary system of today's International Monetary Fund (IMF) and World Bank. During these three decades, since approximately the mid-1970s, we have cheapened the price of goods consumed within the U.S.A. and Europe, by exporting production to regions of the world where production is cheaper.[20] The cheapness is the fruit not only of low wages paid in those other nations, but, more significantly, in the lack of the costs of modern forms of basic economic infrastructure.

Therefore, the financier interests controlling this shift in the world economy demand both savagely lower wages for the general populations of the nations to which production has fled, but they also insist upon the suppression of the cost of providing modern basic economic infrastructure in these new markets, while destroying the productive basis in formerly industrialized powers such as those of the U.S.A. and Europe.

In the meantime, in the attempt of Europe and the U.S.A. to compete with the cheaper production they have engendered in nations with much lower standards of household income, the governments of Europe, the U.S.A., and others, have connived to—in effect—slash their own economic throats, by pushing the prices of labor and investment in infrastructure, down toward "Third World" levels, while, at the same time, driving the prices of goods produced abroad lower, and lower, and still lower, by transferring production from already poor nations of the cheap labor markets, toward nations with the worst imaginable conditions of national life.

As a result of this practice of so-called "globalization," the potential population-density of the planet is being driven toward levels far below the present level of world population. Globalization is, therefore, the practice of genocide, as in Africa, but also on an increasingly global scale.

Much could be said and written of the minds and morals of those influential circles who have concocted and foisted that policy of practice upon our planet. However, for the moment, let us treat this as a scientific fact, as a matter of manifest and massive foolishness, rather than evil intentions.

If this trend, called "globalization," were to be continued, we would reach a critical point, a phase-shift, of self-accelerating physical economic decline globally, at which the potential (e.g., "sustainable") population of the planet would decline to approximately the present population of China, or much less, within a generation or so. Look at the role of investment in basic economic infrastructure in that perspective. Already, throughout most of the world, including the U.S.A. itself, human life itself is becoming very cheap, with that price dropping at a currently accelerating rate. If this continues, a point of phase-shift will be soon reached, at which the level of population will also begin to collapse, and that at an accelerating rate.

---

20. In the U.S.A., for example, the net physical standard of household income of the lower eighty percentile of the population, has fallen rather continuously since approximately 1977. Since the U.S.A. has been incapable of reaching "third world" conditions within its present population-stock, it now imports masses of extremely poor as both legal and illegal immigrants from below its borders.

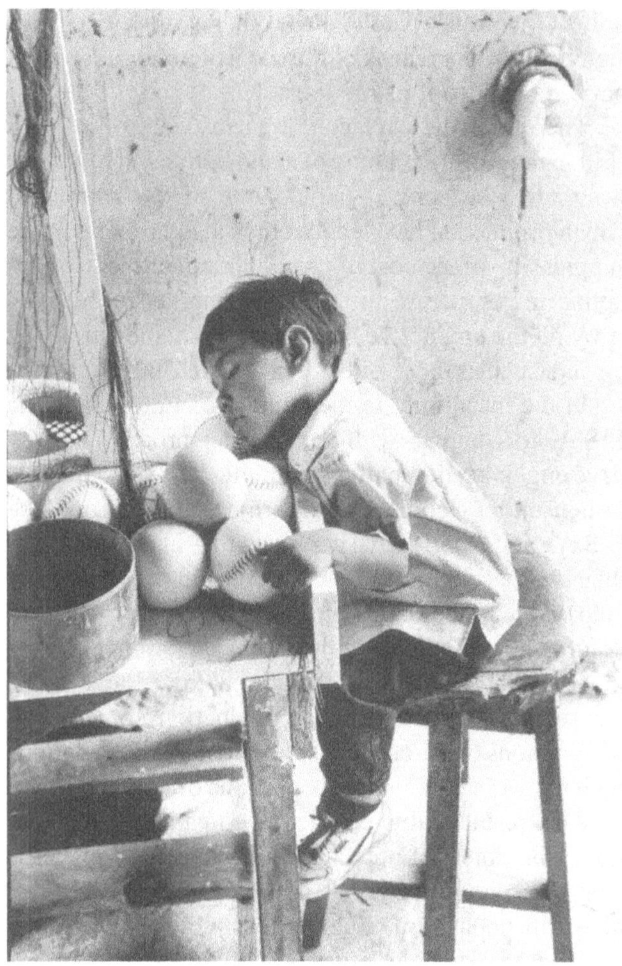

Globalization in Honduras. "As a result of this practice of so-called 'globalization,' the potential population-density of the planet is being driven toward levels far below the present level of world population. Globalization is, therefore, the practice of genocide, as in Africa, but also on an increasingly global scale."

All of this global downturn has been concentrated within the most recent four decades, since about the time Harold Wilson assumed the post of Prime Minister of the United Kingdom, since about the time Zbigniew Brzezinski emitted his late 1960s draft for a "technetronic revolution," since about the time of the eruption of the ultra-decadent "68ers" of the "rock-drug-sex counterculture" and that decadent culture's popular fads of LSD, marijuana, and the like.[21] This change,

which was first implemented, most notably, in the economies of Europe and the Americas as the highly touted "cultural paradigm-shift" of the recent four decades, is the key to understanding how once powerful and increasingly prosperous nations, such as those of North America and Europe, have also willfully destroyed themselves during the course of these four decades to date, and have gone so far into lunacy as largely praising themselves for making this change.

Otherwise, the pattern of "globalization" which I have just summarily described so, can be studied usefully from a different vantage-point, that of Vernadsky's notion of the Noösphere.

The level of the productive powers of labor achieved through technological progress, is not determined solely by the quality of the technology expressed by the process of farming or manufacture. The productive powers of labor expressed in the process of production of a product for market, are largely, even chiefly determined by the role of the basic economic infrastructure provided as the environment of the acts of production of consumable objects purchased. This basic economic infrastructure is expressed both as the necessary environment of production itself, and as the necessary environment of the population engaged in that production.

When those factors are taken into account, cheaper labor in so-called developing nations is not actually a means for lowering the net physical cost of maintaining the world at a present level of potential relative population-density.

One source of complications which tend to mask the physical realities of "outsourcing," is the difference between current price and the price of the same goods produced and sold under conditions in which the economies of the world taken as a whole were actually engaged in long-term net growth, as tended to be the case during the first two decades in post-war Europe and the Americas, for example. That earlier experience must be compared with what is now shown to have been a long wave of net decline in those regions, a presently persisting decline which began at varying points, from case to case, during the more recent four decades.

The reality of the past four decades begins to be demonstrated forcibly when we take into account the

---

21. This plunge into decadence, while triggered by the U.S. war in Indo-China and other factors of the middle to late 1960s, was not so much a product of the 1960s, as it was a reflection of the impact of the influence of the counter-cultural Congress for Cultural Freedom on the education and other relevant circumstances of life of the children and youth of the 1950s, especially the suburban population of that time.

Vietnam was the detonator, but the 1950s influence of the Congress for Cultural Freedom was the explosive cultural charge which was exploded as the "68er" syndrome. The hypocrisy of the parents of 1950s suburbia matured as what was, potentially, the culturally fatal sophistry all too typical of their children, the "68ers."

loss of modern production facilities, the falling physical standard of living of the population of a nation considered as a whole, and the rising demand, that costs which nations formerly paid, are being cut, cut, cut, and cut again. It is as if governments, such as that of the Second Administration under U.S. President George W. Bush, Jr., were telling their people, "We are reaching the point that we can no longer afford to keep you alive." The savage cuts in pensions and healthcare in the U.S.A. and western Europe, are typical of this morbid trend.

What we have termed "basic economic infrastructure" is not only an essential part of the cost of production of a nation's salable output of commodities. The level of technological development and physical capital-intensity of investment in infrastructure is itself a multiplier of the productivity of labor employed in the fabrication and distribution of agricultural and manufactured products.

Step back one step. The lowering of the physical cost of production of goods through scientific and technological progress occurs as much in the form this progress is incorporated in investment in basic economic infrastructure, as in the direct costs of production and distribution of manufactured and distributed agricultural and manufacturing product.

Thus, by shifting production to poorer countries, while allowing the rot and discard of infrastructure and production in nations such as those of North America and Europe, we have lowered the net per-capita output of the world as a whole, by lowering the net level of technology expressed as both basic economic infrastructure and the production of marketable goods. We wreck the nations, such as the U.S.A. and Europe, which had the highest relative concentration of investment in maintenance and improvement of productive technology and related basic economic infrastructure, while relying upon production by a small fraction of the total population in so-called developing economies, "developing economies" in which the technological level of production and standard of living is typically low, even very low. What it has become fashionable to describe as "globalization" has been a process of what has become a factually undeniable collapse of the productivity of the planet considered as a whole.

Since the useful physical life-span of much of the basic economic infrastructure on which modern life depends, runs in the order of between one and two generations, the nearly four decades of increasing neglect of

replacement and repair of basic economic infrastructure has brought much of the world, North America and Europe most notably, to a much lower level of productive potential than during the 1960s. The time has come at which worn-out infrastructure, and lost investment in modern agriculture and industry, must be replaced rapidly, on a vast scale, or there will be a sudden collapse of productive potential to levels far below that prevalent up to this moment. This approach to the closing phase of a long-term capital cycle, in relevant sections of the world, now defines a precipice for the world economy as a whole during the times immediately before us. Unless there is a sudden, drastic shift back to heavy investment in basic economic infrastructure, the apparently slower long-term decline in economy experienced during recent decades will soon be jolted by a relatively precipitous rate of physical decline, even a collapse.

Economy and the Noösphere

Now, reconsider the following from among those excerpts from Vernadsky's 1935 paper which I quoted at the outset of this report. Reconsider the formulation, now slightly modified: *It,* cognition, *defines the way in which society (i.e., the Noösphere) organizes the flow of both abiotic and organic materials which it absorbs, uses, and discharges.* Compare my own views with those stated by Vernadsky for the case of the Biosphere.

For this purpose, I shall interpolate some restatements, as comments, here, of some of the points I have made above. By repeating them in this way, we may hope to make clearer to the reader what I have already stated on this matter above.

For example, quoting and slightly paraphrasing Vernadsky:

"If this structure is called a mechanism, it would be a special, very peculiar mechanism, a continuously changing mechanism—a dynamic equilibrium—never reaching a state strictly identical in the past and in the future. At every moment of the past and of the future time the equilibrium is different but closely resembling. It contains so many components, so many parameters, so many independent variables, that no strict and precise return of some state in its previous form is possible. An idea of it may be given by comparing it to the dynamic equilibrium of the living organism itself. In this sense it is more convenient to speak of the *organized state,* rather than of the *mechanism* of the biosphere."

Let us apply this image to the economy as I have

described it in the immediately preceding pages. Instead of regarding an economy as charlatans such as Mandeville, François Quesnay, Adam Smith, and Jeremy Bentham have done, consider an economy as a kind of organism. This time, consider it as an organism of the Noösphere, rather than the Biosphere.

"Life," in this case the principle of creative reason, "is continuously and immutably connected with the" Noösphere, and also the subsumed "biosphere. It is inseparable from the latter materially and energetically. The living organisms are connected with the biosphere through their nutrition, breathing, reproduction, and metabolism. This connection may be precisely and fully expressed quantitatively by the migration of atoms from the biosphere to the living organism and back again—*the biogenic migration of atoms*. The more energetic the biogenic migration of the atoms, the more intense is life," or, in this case, cognition. "It," in this case, of economy, "is nearly dying out or hardly flickering in the latest phases of life, the importance of which in the organized state has not yet been evaluated, but should not be overlooked.

"The biogenic migration of atoms," or in this case, the materials produced and consumed by the integrated economic process of society as a whole, "comprises the whole of the biosphere, and is the fundamental natural phenomenon characteristic of it.

"In the aspect of historical time—within a decamyriad, a hundred thousand years,—there is no natural phenomenon in the biosphere more geologically powerful than," in this case, human "life."

"The chief geological importance of these masses of substance embraced by life," in this case physical economy, "that seem small when compared to the mass of the biosphere, is connected with their exclusively great energetic activity.

"This property of the living substance," in this case, cognition, "having nothing equal to it in the substance of the planet, not only at the given moment, but also in the aspect of geological time, completely distinguishes it from any other earthly substance and makes the distinction between the living and inert substance of the planet quite sharp, the more so that all the living is derived from the living. The connection between the living and the inert substance of the biosphere is indissoluble and material within the geological time—of the order of a milliard of years, and is maintained exclusively by the biogenic migration of atoms. Abiogenesis is not known in any form of its manifestation. Practi-

cally, the naturalist cannot overlook in his work this empirically precise deduction from a scientific observation of nature, even if he does not agree with it due to his religious or philosophically religious premises."

"The whole work of the Laboratory," in this case, my discoveries and their use in economy, "is based on such a structure of the" Noösphere, "on the existence of an impassable sharp, materially energetical boundary between the" cognitive "and" non-cognitive "substance."

"It is necessary to dwell on this point, since it appears to me that in this question there is a vagueness of thought, which impedes scientific work." Such is the situation in the practice of economy by nations today.

"We do not proceed here beyond exact empiric observation, the deductions from which are obligatory for the scientist and as a matter of fact for every one; it is on this observation that he not only *can* but *must* base his work. These deductions may possibly be explained differently, but in the form of *empiric generalization* they are to be taken into consideration in science, for an empiric generalization is neither a scientific theory, nor a scientific hypothesis, nor else a working hypothesis. This generalized expression of scientifically established facts is logically as obligatory as the scientific facts themselves—if it has been logically correctly formulated." It is the same for economy today.

"The sharp material energetic distinction of the living organisms in the biosphere—of the living substance of the biosphere—from any other substance of the biosphere penetrates the whole field of phenomena studied in biogeochemistry." It is the same for the Noösphere.

Here, the application of Dirichlet's Principle to the physical processes of economy shines forth. For this purpose, we shall replace the use of the term "life," by "cognition." Both terms are cognates of *creation*. One as applied to the principle expressed by living processes; the second as a higher order of creativity, cognition as defined by man's experimentally validatable discovery of a universal physical, or equivalent principle. In place of Vernadsky's "the biogenic migration of atoms," we have "the cognitive migration of materials."

If we apply that standard for the healthy, normal state of the Noösphere to the evidence of Earth's economy during the recent forty years, especially since the election of President Richard Nixon, we would be obliged to describe the political-economic doctrines of practice of the U.S. economy, and also that of Europe, since that time as clinically insane. The criteria of the cheapest price and highest rate of financial profit have not only failed, but have shown themselves the worst imaginable sort of threat to the future of the human species, and economists of that persuasion defined as a failed species.

Let us, therefore, take the cited 1935 criteria of Vernadsky for the Biosphere as a standard of comparison. Let us adopt the intention to investigate the nature of those pathological features of the recent three and a half decades of the U.S. economy from that vantage-point. We proceed as follows.

The difficulty we face in treating the subject of human creativity, as Vernadsky faced a similar problem of method in his defining the Biosphere, is that, just as the principle of life which is expressed by living processes, is not found within the province of biochemistry, the power which orders the creative powers of the individual human mind are not biological processes as such. In both instances, we are confronted by something which is universal, and physically efficient, but intangible to the senses.

It is not accidental that problems of this type could not be addressed effectively by an Euler, Lagrange, or other empiricists. When these gentlemen set out to deny the existence of the infinitesimal in Leibniz's catenary-cued calculus of the universal principle of physical least action, they eliminated attention to those discontinuities which betray the presence of a universal physical principle, principles of a type which Classical Platonic Greek science found in Archytas' construction of a solution for the doubling of the cube. Such knowledge can not be reached by any ordinary inductive method, certainly not by the methods of the reductionist inductive-deductive "sciences."

We can, indeed, often recognize the presence or absence of what is properly named human creativity once we have the hang of conducting such investigations, but our knowledge of the principle of intellectual creativity is limited to a kind of evidence similar to Vernadsky's reference to the Biosphere. Hundreds of thousands of years' accumulation of the fossils of the Biosphere, approximate universality in ways which permit systematic investigation of the way in which a principle of life expresses its footprints. In human creativity, the fossils of physical scientific progress work to similar effect.

The work of such outstanding Renaissance figures as Brunelleschi and Leonardo da Vinci has pin-pointed elements of discovery in artistic composition which, fortunately, if seemingly coincidentally, are verifiable as such by physical-scientific methods. When the cross-voice relations within Classical compositions in J.S. Bach and such followers as W.A. Mozart and Beethoven are adduced by demonstration in performance, creativity can be precisely defined in the medium of musical composition. In general, when the forms of ambiguity which are rightly presented as ironies are shown to point to a verifiable truth not otherwise accessible to conventional use of language, a similar proof can be adduced.

In language, as in art, just as life as such seems inaccessible to the senses, it is generally impossible to convey important discoveries by literal use of an established habit in employment of a language. Only a creative intellect can discover the existence of creativity. Creativity can be communicated only by prompting the activation of the creative powers specific to the individual human mind. However, even the dumbest of beasts, or of U.S. Presidents could feel the force unleashed by that human creativity. Thus, it is a fine point of Mosaic theology, and the theology of Plato's *Timaeus*, that only man can know the unseen God, although the universe must feel His effects.

In other words, can we know the principles of a sane economy by applying the methods which Vernadsky applied to the Biosphere, to the economy defined as an expression of the Noösphere? The question is thus posed: would we then be using the model of the Noösphere as a trick for understanding the economic process, or is it also the case, that knowledge of the physical economy, viewed in this way, is indispensable for probing the Noösphere with a precision lacking in the methods actually developed in any record of the work by Vernadsky?

3. Ancient and Modern Society Today

The most significant scientific problem to be faced in efforts to define society for these purposes, is that the modern society has systemic characteristics which do not exist in ancient and medieval forms of European society. Moreover, the prevalent practices of national economies today are an awkward mixing of modern economy with a superimposed relic of medieval society.

The chief common problem of today's study and application of a habit called "economics," is that the prevalent, world-wide view of the subject itself has been shaped by that tradition of Venetian financier-aristocratic usury whose product is known today as the intrinsically imperial Anglo-Dutch Liberal system. This view is typified by Mandeville's Enron-like promise that great good can come only from the unhampered proliferation of small-minded private acts of evil. What, then, if we put aside the superstition that the interest earned on loan of money is the Cain-raising Adam and Eve of economy? Why should we tolerate the existence of a creature which has shown itself the author of such pernicious doings as wild money has often done, as with the pestilence of financial-derivatives speculation today, and that on a tremendous scale, now an absolutely unpayable sum, many times greater than the total annual product of the planet as a whole?

This Anglo-Dutch Liberal financial system on which the fanatical doctrines of our contemporary monetarists are premised, is most explicitly a relic of a form of medieval society known as the ultramontane system, established as an alliance of the medieval Venetian financier-oligarchical system with the Norman chivalry. Like ancient society, medieval ultramontane systems subordinated the great majority of the population to the status of human cattle, defining social relations in a way echoed by the argument on behalf of the dogma of *laissez-faire* of the Physiocrat François Quesnay. Quesnay's argument, from which the British East India Company's Adam Smith derived his "free trade" dogma, was, as I have already emphasized above, an echo of the doctrine of the Olympian Zeus from **Prometheus Bound**, insisting that mankind not be permitted to have knowledge of the use of "fire"—i.e., universal physical principles.

In the contrary form of society, the modern sovereign nation-state republic otherwise named a *commonwealth*, the principle of organization is called *the general welfare principle*. In this organization of society, the ideas corresponding to fundamental principles of science circulate more or less freely and abundantly in society. Thus, in the typical ancient and medieval society, the noëtic principle is not the characteristic mode of organization of the society as a whole, whereas, in that modern European sovereign republic which is sometimes referred to as a commonwealth, the noëtic principle is the characteristic form of action within the social process.

Although the principle of the republic committed to the promotion of the general welfare is ancient knowledge, as the cases of Solon of Athens, Socrates, and Plato typify this, the constitution of nation-states based upon the principle of progress in the promotion of the general welfare dates from the Fifteenth-Century Renaissance and such exemplary cases as France under Louis XI and the application of Louis's principle by England's Henry VII.

The situation became complex with the resurgence of the power of the Venetian financier-oligarchy as a result of the Ottoman conquest of Constantinople. From the expulsion of the Jews from Spain by the Inquisition in 1492, until the 1648 Treaty of Westphalia, the Venetian faction used religious warfare and persecution, as in Karl Rove's Flagellant-like political following in the U.S.A. today, as a weapon to divide the emerging modern European nations against one another. The weakening of the power of Venice as a state power during the Seventeenth Century led to the continuation of the Venetian model of quasi-imperial rule by the Dutch and English India Company models based on the special doctrine, called empiricism, of Venice's Paolo Sarpi, a doctrine which has dominated world finance, and the popular ideology of Europe and other locations, since the February 1763 Treaty of Paris where London's imperial supremacy was first established in the interest of the British East India Company at that time.

The model modern form of sovereign nation-state republic for today was established with the 1789 U.S. Federal Constitution; but, the chain-reaction effects of the French Revolution and Napoleonic rule and ruin, combined with Anglo-Dutch Liberal corruption, isolated the young U.S.A. for an extended period, until the U.S.'s emergence as a world power during 1863-1876 and its emergence as a leading world power under President Franklin Roosevelt.

Thus, we have two leading "models" of European-style economies today. The Anglo-Dutch Liberal imperial system of international financier-oligarchical hegemony, into which the U.S.A. itself has been, unfortunately, significantly assimilated, versus the true modern nation-state system typified by the often misused principles on which the U.S. Constitutional system was founded. In the latter system, we have the basis for what might be termed a Vernadskyian model of Noösphere republic. The process of "globalization" which is threatening the extinction of civilization today, is a product of that Liberal tradition.

The complication arising between the two systems,

the American System and the Anglo-Dutch Liberal system, is the fact that the role of technological progress has persisted until now as a determining economic and also military strategic factor, as the U.S. demonstrated during the 1939-1945 war. This factor has been such that nations under the Anglo-Dutch Liberal model, which are naturally better fit by ideology and temperament for a quasi-feudal form of society, than a modern, scientifically progressive agro-industrial culture, have nonetheless been unable, until now, to free themselves from a strategic compulsion to maintain society on the basis of a commitment to continuation of scientific-technological progress. The attempt to consolidate the form of imperialism called "globalization," is an effort to rid the world, once and for all, of everything which modern European civilization had accomplished.

Thus, we must face the ugly truth, that the post-1964 rise of the "rock-drug-sex youth-counterculture" and the insurgence of "environmentalism," represent an effort of the neo-Venetian, Anglo-Dutch Liberal interest to free itself from the strategic threat which scientific-technological progress constitutes for an attempted continuation of financier-oligarchical hegemony.

Since 1789, the principal alternative to the Anglo-Dutch Liberal model has been what is known as the American System of political-economy, a system which is implicit in the composition of the U.S. Federal constitutional republic.

If the U.S. now comes back to its senses, pulling back from the terrible holocaust which the architects of the American oligarch George Pratt Shultz's Bush II Administration have unleashed, we have one last chance to stop the plunge toward global Hell. If we succeed in doing that in the U.S.A. itself—with whatever cooperation we might find for that noble .enterprise—the mission of a community of perfectly sovereign nation-states will be to use the U.S. revolutionary model of 1789 as the rallying point for a system of international cooperation among sovereign states, a system we might have had but for President Franklin Roosevelt's most untimely death.

Then, the ideas associated with Vernadsky's conception of Biosphere and Noösphere will provide a needed added guidance for new global forms of cooperation among sovereign commonwealths. Then, the ideas expressed and otherwise reflected in the foregoing pages will become a possible reality for mankind as a whole.

FIDELIO

Journal of Poetry, Science, and Statecraft

From the first issue, dated Winter 1992, featuring Lyndon LaRouche on "The Science of Music: The Solution to Plato's Paradox of 'The One and the Many,'" to the final issue of Spring/Summer 2006, a "Symposium on Edgar Allan Poe and the Spirit of the American Revolution," *Fidelio* magazine gave voice to the Schiller Institute's intention to create a new Golden Renaissance.

The title of the magazine, is taken from Beethoven's great opera, which celebrates the struggle for political freedom over tyranny. *Fidelio* was founded at the time that LaRouche and several of his close associates were unjustly imprisoned, as was the opera's Florestan, whose character was based on the American Revolutionary hero, the French General, Marquis de Lafayette.

Each issue of *Fidelio*, throughout its 14-year lifespan, remained faithful to its initial commitment, and offered original writings by LaRouche and his associates, on matters of, what the poet Percy Byssche Shelley identified as, "profound and impassioned conceptions respecting man and nature."

Back issues are now available for purchase through the Schiller Institute website:
http://schillerinstitute.org/about/order_form.html

9 781985 760660